A
BUTTERFLY
NOTEBOOK

A Butterfly Notebook

Douglas Hammersley

The Book Guild Ltd
Sussex, England

First published in Great Britain in 2003 by
The Book Guild Ltd
25 High Street
Lewes, East Sussex
BN7 2LU

Typesetting in Adobe Berling by Hammersley Graphics

Origination, printing and binding in Singapore
under the supervision of MRM Graphics Ltd, Winslow, Bucks

A catalogue record for this book is available from
The British Library.

ISBN 1 85776 995 3

CONTENTS

INTRODUCTION

This book has two intentions. First, it is designed to be a pictorial celebration of the sheer beauty of butterflies; with the hope that this collection of paintings may arouse in those readers with only a passing interest in butterflies, a delight in seeing examples of their wonderful diversity of colour and design. To those who already know their butterflies, perhaps the pictures may reveal some extra insight into the anatomy of the species illustrated, especially in the case of the smaller butterflies which have been enlarged to show details not easily seen in the field.

The second intention lies in the text. Here I have deliberately adopted a narrative style in order to give some idea of the excitement and vicissitudes of butterfly hunting, rather than present factual details of the life-cycles and present status of each butterfly, species-by-species. Where I have included such facts it has been because I felt them to be of interest in the case of that particular butterfly.

Although these pages may be used to aid identification of the sixty species illustrated, they are in no sense offered as a textbook or as a field guide. Indeed, the book's format is not intended for the pocket. This is more a book for visual enjoyment; a book for the browser, who perhaps wishes to brighten a winter evening by slowly studying the pages and dreaming of summer!

I began drawing and painting butterflies on my retirement from a career as a medical artist. For thirty-two years between 1950 and 1982, I worked as an illustrator and graphic designer in the service of medical education. During those years, I produced many hundreds of drawings for surgical textbooks, and artwork for teaching displays, medical films and television. Through this work I came to recognise the beauty of living structures, the marvellous design of the human body and its component parts. What better way of continuing this study of living forms than turning to butterflies, surely some of the most beautiful designs in all creation.

I soon learned that, not only was there great pleasure to be derived from my efforts to reproduce the wonderful shapes and colours of butterflies, but there were new sources of delight to be found in watching them in their natural environment. The exhilaration of finding a species I had not seen before; the fascination of watching their behaviour; the way that their dancing flight enlivens the woodland scene. All this increased my interest and spurred me on to learn more about butterflies.

I had tried sketching butterflies in the field but soon came to realise the difficulty of trying to catch their patterns and postures with a pencil. I realised that I would have to use a camera to get the detail I wished to record. This aroused a further interest, that of collecting pictures not only of the appearance of the butterflies, but also recording their behaviour: their courtship manoeuvres, mating, egg-laying, feeding, and even showing butterflies being preyed upon by spiders or parasitic mites. Using fast film, a high-speed flash and a macro lens which could give me life-size pictures, I found that I could freeze their motion and occasionally photograph butterflies in flight.

You may be inclined to ask: why, if you find photographs so effective in illustrating butterflies, do you go to the trouble of making paintings of them? Here, I bring to mind my years as a medical artist when I found that, very often, drawings and paintings served to communicate more powerfully than photographs. The camera is not selective; it will record everything seen through the lens. In contrast, the artist is interpretive, and can emphasise what is important and discard what may be irrelevant or distracting.

By using photographs as reference pictures, in the manner of a sketchbook, I have been able to remove a distracting background, or 'repair' the tattered wing of an injured butterfly to show it as a perfect specimen, and add emphasis and completeness to what may be half-hidden or ambiguous in the photograph.

Here I would like to stress that, throughout this book, my paintings are based only on my own photographs and on no others. Indeed, many of the photographs were taken with a specific group of paintings in mind.

I had hoped to illustrate all the butterflies on the list of British species, but for various reasons this was not possible; illness and advancing age were the most obvious ones. In my late seventies, I do not feel able to search the northern hilltops to find the Mountain Ringlet, although last year I managed to scramble about the Spanish Pyrenees, thanks to the assistance of Paul Cardy, my guide and mentor.

I am aware of some glaring omissions besides the Mountain Ringlet: the Black Hairstreak, Brown Hairstreak, Large Heath, Large Blue and Chequered Skipper are missing. As a make-weight, I have included a few of the more spectacular European butterflies, especially those that in former years were found in Britain. It has been my policy to give each species more or less equal space to show its structure in detail. Thus, all butterflies are shown to be about the same size when, of course, they differ greatly in their dimensions in life. The Small Blue would barely cover the thumbnail, whereas the Swallowtail would cover most of the palm of the hand. To indicate their correct sizes, I have included life-size pictures of each species.

In addition to the pleasure I gained from photographing and painting butterflies, my experience was enriched by joining others in recording them. In 1985 I joined the British Butterfly Conservation Society (now Butterfly Conservation) and took part in various butterfly monitoring schemes, collecting records of sightings in my garden, from visits to woodland and fens in the neighbourhood, and from weekly transect walks along selected rides in West Harling Forest near my home.

With my wife Joan, I made many trips to find butterflies in Britain and Europe. Joan tolerated my obsession with butterflies, but she always insisted that, during our travels, time would be set aside to follow her interests in architecture and history. As these subjects also interested me, both pursuits were followed, and peace prevailed!

I have been encouraged to persevere with butterfly painting by my sons, Mike and Roger, who have given me fresh impetus when returning to the task after long lapses. They have also made helpful suggestions concerning the contents of this book. In the early days, my friend Peter West was responsible for kindling my interest in butterflies, and assisted me by locating butterfly sites. More recently, I have valued the opinions of fellow-members of the Thetford Natural History Society, members of the Norfolk and Norwich Naturalists' Society, and members of the Suffolk Branch of Butterfly Conservation. Mike Hall, the author of *An Atlas of Norfolk Butterflies 1984–1988* and the present Norfolk County Moth Officer, has helped me in several ways, and I am glad to have been able to reciprocate his kindness by making illustrations for his publications.

Most of all, I shall forever be grateful for the loving assistance of Joan, who died on the eighth day of the new millennium, ending a wonderful companionship lasting fifty-four years.

1

Papilionidae:

SWALLOWTAILS & APOLLO

SWALLOWTAIL

SCARCE SWALLOWTAIL

APOLLO

SWALLOWTAIL

My first sighting of the Swallowtail occurred during the morning of 25 June 1984 when I spotted two of these elegant insects flying quickly along the northern edge of Lake Bohinj in Slovenia. They were moving in an easterly direction helped by a following breeze; their flight was not very graceful, indeed they reminded one of a pair of racing yachts pitching and tossing in a lively sea. There was no hope of photographing them. At that time Joan and I were enjoying a short break away from our home in Northumberland. Less than a year later we had moved to live in Norfolk where the only remaining colonies of the British Swallowtails *(subspecies britannicus)* survive in several river valley fens in the Broads. Broadland lies within easy reach of our home in the south of the county and soon I was able to satisfy my wish to see Swallowtails at close quarters. My first photographs of them were taken along the southern edge of Heigham Sound which lies adjacent to Hickling Broad. Here I watched about fifteen of these magnificent creatures feeding on the nectar of ragged robin and creeping thistle flowerheads. They fluttered continuously while feeding, keeping a tenuous balance among the flowers, but I was able to freeze their motion by using high-speed flash.

The following year, at the same place, I found individual male Swallowtails basking in the sunshine along the rough pathway by the Sound. These were spaced at intervals and, now and then, one would ascend vigorously in defence of its particular territory. Some had damaged tails, indicating that they had been attacked by birds or other predators. The fact that the damage occurred to their nether parts illustrates the value of their 'back-to-front' mimicry which enables them to protect their vital parts by displaying a 'false head' at the trailing edge of their wings. The large red spot on the inner edge of the hindwing leads the predator to believe that this is an eye, and that the tails are antennae! This can be visualised by looking at the top picture.

The Swallowtail is widespread throughout Europe. I have found it on high mountain meadows in Austria, Italy and Spain, and in coastal areas where I found my best 'photo opportunity'. This was on the lovely island of Mljet, off the Adriatic coast of Croatia, where my wife and I stayed during June 1987. Just a few yards from our hotel, on the northwest tip of the island, was a patch of waste ground bearing a mass of wildflowers. For hours on end a succession of large butterflies, mainly Swallowtails, Cardinals and Cleopatras gorged on the nectar-rich thistles. This time, photography was easy and I was able to take many frame-filling shots – two of which were used as references for the paintings opposite.

These European Swallowtails *(subspecies gorganus)* closely resemble their English cousins, the main difference being seen in the greater distribution of dark scales in *britannicus*, especially along the veins of the upper wing surfaces. This gives a more pronounced wing pattern and the butterfly as a whole a somewhat darker look than its continental counterpart.

SWALLOWTAIL

Papilio machaon

Mljet, Yugoslavia
26 June

♂ Lifesize

Mljet, Yugoslavia
23 June

Papilio machaon ssp. britannicus
Heigham Sound, Norfolk
8 June

SCARCE SWALLOWTAIL

Iphiclides podalirius

Mljet, Yugoslavia
27 June

Male, lifesize

Mljet, Yugoslavia
27 June

Spanish Pyrenees
22 June

SCARCE SWALLOWTAIL

Despite its name, the Scarce Swallowtail is not particularly scarce, although its numbers have rapidly diminished in certain parts of its range due to loss of suitable habitat where intensive agriculture has developed. In general its distribution across central and southern Europe is about the same as that of the Swallowtail, although it is not present in the colder regions such as Denmark, Scandinavia and the British Isles. It is usually found in open places where there are flowers, in orchards and scrubby woodland.

Its appearance is even more spectacular than the Swallowtail, with its prominent black stripes making a dazzle pattern on the forewings. Like the Swallowtail, its hindwing 'eyes' and long tails give it the protection of 'back-to-front' mimicry. The unusually large wing area, in proportion to its body size, provides the Scarce Swallowtail with the ability to glide freely and yet make a sudden high-speed dash to chase away intruding butterflies when patrolling its territory. I was able to watch this patrolling activity in June 2001 when I was standing in a small area of wooded heathland in the foothills of the Spanish Pyrenees. Here a fine, fresh-looking Scarce Swallowtail was regularly patrolling a roughly triangular area, each leg of which was about 50 metres. At the end of each 'circuit' the butterfly alighted on the upper branch of a rather scraggy kermes oak. The object of these patrols may have been defence of territory or seeking a mate.

My best chance to get photographs of the Scarce Swallowtail occurred in June 1987 during our sojourn on the Adriatic island of Mljet when Joan and I, tiring of sitting in the harbour area watching the cruise ships disgorging sightseers (not to mention watching the nudists cavorting on the nearby islet of Pomestak) decided to walk inland and look for butterflies. We walked south, following the road to Govedari. The day was very hot and we had the sun in our eyes as we climbed inland. We became increasingly uncomfortable and breathless as we trudged along. Should we turn back? After all, we were both in our mid-sixties! I stopped to examine the large, solitary flower of a milk thistle which was growing at the roadside. Suddenly, a Scarce Swallowtail landed on the thistlehead and immediately began feeding on the nectar. So preoccupied was the butterfly that it allowed me to get a close-up photograph. We managed to reach the top of the hill where, to our delight, we found a group of Scarce Swallowtails nectaring on these thistles. I took many photographs. Feeling amply rewarded for our effort, we turned back to our hotel for a refreshing drink.

APOLLO

The Apollo can be found in most mountain ranges in Europe stretching from Spain to the Balkans and northwards to southern Norway and Finland. This exquisite butterfly has long been enthusiastically sought after by collectors, resulting in its extinction in some places and numerical decline elsewhere. Thankfully, it is now protected by law in many European countries, though a good deal of illegal collecting still takes place. The Apollo breeds on rocky hillsides at altitudes of up to 2000 metres where various species of *Sedum*, plants on which the caterpillars feed, cling to crevices in the rock face. Adult Apollos feed in nearby high meadows where they take nectar from such plants as knapweed and thistles.

John Feltwell, in his fascinating book *The Natural History of Butterflies*, describes how the Apollo is able to defend itself from predators in three ways: visually, by flashing its red eye spot markings on its hindwings; and audibly, from rubbing the undersides of its hindwings against its resting place or by scraping the back of its legs against the base of the wing, thus producing a hissing sound.

Over the years, I have had much frustration during attempts to find the Apollo, and I have taken many rides in cable cars, on chairlifts and funicular railways to mountain tops in Italy and Austria, and walked many a mountain path without even a glimpse of one. Typical of my disappointments is noted in an entry in my butterfly logbook: 'Kirchberg-in-Tirol, 1st July 1986 – An accident resulting in a torn Achilles tendon prevented further butterfly-watching'. This note explains another lost opportunity for me to find an Apollo. This 'accident' was the result of a wine-induced exuberance whilst leading a round-the-hotel conga dance when I attempted to emulate Rudolf Nureyev by leaping in the air – and landing ungracefully. The following morning, instead of butterfly hunting on a nearby mountain, having been assured that Apollos were to be found there, I was hobbling about on crutches and spent the next seven days confined to the hotel garden! Not until fifteen years later did I get an Apollo in my camera viewfinder.

It was on 21 June 2001, while on a natural history holiday in the Spanish Pyrenees, that I saw my first Apollo. I certainly wouldn't have known where to find Apollos but for the expert knowledge of my guide, Paul Cardy. I was able to take three photographs – one a close-up and two rather indifferent long shots, from which I produced the paintings reproduced opposite.

APOLLO

Parnassius apollo

Female
Spanish Pyrenees
21st June

Lifesize

Female
Spanish Pyrenees
21st June

Male
Spanish Pyrenees
21st June

2
Pieridae:

WHITES & YELLOWS

LARGE WHITE
BLACK-VEINED WHITE
SMALL WHITE
GREEN-VEINED WHITE
BATH WHITE
ORANGE TIP
CLOUDED YELLOW
BRIMSTONE
WOOD WHITE

LARGE WHITE

T he Large White, *Pieris brassicae*, (commonly known as the Cabbage White), is a very successful butterfly. It is widespread throughout Britain and Europe and very numerous, although its numbers may suffer from time to time due to the use of pesticides or through parasitism and viral infection.

In Britain we can expect to see Large Whites in our gardens from mid-April, followed by a second generation emerging in midsummer. In some years numbers may swell due to migrant Large Whites arriving from France. The success of this butterfly is due in part to the abundance of its food plants, but also to its ability to resist predation. Both caterpillars and adult butterflies are protected from predation by birds and spiders due to the poisons in their bodies which give them a very unpleasant taste and smell. These poisons are derived from mustard oils occurring in the food plants such as cabbages, sprouts and nasturtium ingested by the caterpillars.

When speaking about butterflies to gardeners, I invariably show a slide which shows, in stark close-up, a cabbage leaf being devoured by a mass of Large White caterpillars. This usually produces a groan from the audience. I then suggest to them that they should be gratified that a female Large White had taken the trouble to carefully examine their cabbage leaf, testing it for quality before laying a batch of eggs. Needless to say, the gardeners are not impressed!

I do not grow vegetables in my garden so Large Whites spend little time there, particularly the female butterflies which quickly pass on to find more suitable places to lay their eggs. Only in the late summer do Large Whites deign to stop and feed from my buddleia and phlox flowers. However, they sometimes honour me by using my patio as a nuptial couch when I am granted the opportunity to photograph them coupled! On another occasion, in a shaded corner of the garden, I watched a newly-emerged male Large White hanging upside down on a side branch of a plant and slowly stiffening its limp wings as its veins became engorged with circulating blood. I also noted its repeated attempts to join together the two halves of its proboscis into a functional feeding tube and, when this had been achieved, exercising the coiling and uncoiling muscles of the proboscis. This must be an important exercise if the butterfly is to feed and thereby survive.

The paintings show the difference in the upper forewing markings of the sexes. The male has no top surface spots; the female has four.

Lifesize

Male (spring)

Female
East Harling, Norfolk
20th August

Male
East Harling, Norfolk
3rd September

Female
East Harling, Norfolk
20th August

Lifesize

LARGE WHITE

Pieris brassicae

Female (spring)

Male, lifesize

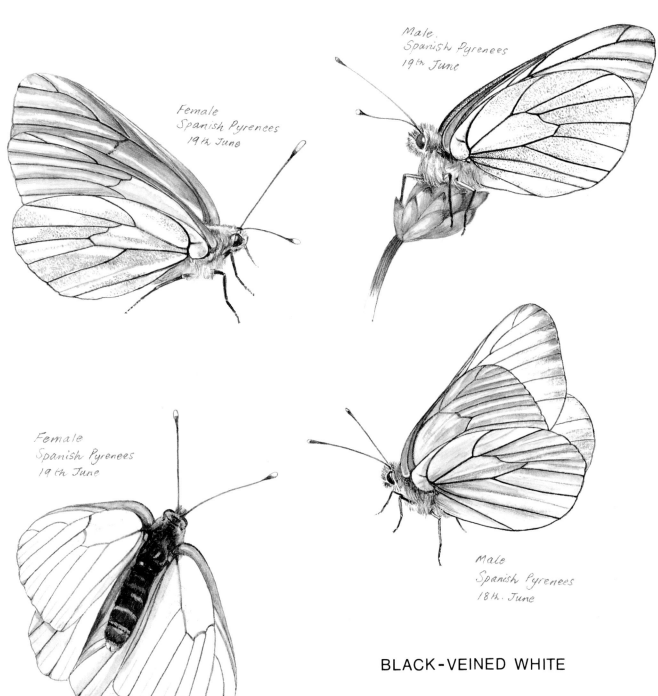

Male.
Spanish Pyrenees
19th June

Female
Spanish Pyrenees
19th June

Female
Spanish Pyrenees
19th June

Male
Spanish Pyrenees
18th. June

BLACK-VEINED WHITE

Aporia crataegi

BLACK-VEINED WHITE

In common with many other butterflies, the scientific name of the Black-veined White, *Aporia crataegi*, indicates its larval food plant *Crataegus monogyna* or hawthorn. A.M. Stewart, writing about the Black-veined White in the 1918 edition of his book *British Butterflies* states: 'This is one of our rarest butterflies, though why it should be so is rather difficult to say. As it feeds upon hawthorn in the larval state the puzzle is all the greater, as a commoner or more widely distributed plant would be hard to find'. These words were written at a time when the Black-veined White was still present in southern England. Alas, it was deemed to be extinct a few years later, and attempts to reintroduce it failed.

The Black-veined White is widespread throughout most of Continental Europe where it feeds on crops of clover and lucerne and a variety of meadow flowers. Its eggs are laid on hawthorn, blackthorn, cherry and plum. It is regarded as a pest by fruit growers as the young caterpillars (which overwinter within a dense, silken web on their host plant) emerge in early spring to feed on the buds and young leaves of the fruit trees.

My first sighting of the Black-veined White occurred while I stood in a queue outside the entrance to the Postojna Caves in Slovenia on 28 June 1984. Three of these butterflies were feeding on the flowers of an overhanging climber just above my head. I was fascinated by the clean design of these insects. Free of any decorative spots or bright colours, and with near-transparent wings displaying the elegant tracery of veins, they struck me as the very epitome of butterfly form.

Generally speaking, I have found the Black-veined White easy to photograph but somewhat disconcerting in the way it can apparently change colour! Throughout its brief life, the butterfly loses its wing scales – especially the female, which tightly grips the male between her wings during mating. This, together with other wing-scale loss caused by brushing against plants and in flying, soon results in the wing surface becoming transparent. When the butterfly is feeding on short meadow flowers against a background of grass it appears to have green wings. This can cause difficulties in obtaining an accurate photographic record of the butterfly's actual colouration. I noticed this when photographing Black-veined Whites in the Pyrenees. Most of my shots showed them as having dark-green segments on their wing surfaces, sometimes in conjunction with brilliant silver patches where the sunlight was reflected. Fortunately, I was able to exclude these aberrations when making paintings based on these photographs.

SMALL WHITE

In common with the Large White, the Small White *(Pieris rapae)* is regarded by many vegetable growers as a pest. Though its attack on the cabbage patch is rather more subtle than that of the Large White, which blatantly lays a batch of up to fifty eggs on the under surface of a brassica leaf, the Small White lays her eggs singly. The resultant leaf-green caterpillar is much less conspicuous than the writhing mass of brightly coloured Large White caterpillars, and the caterpillar of *rapae* has the propensity of boring its way into the centre of the cabbage plant and secretly eating the more tender parts first, moving outwards until the plant is destroyed, or the caterpillar sated.

The Small White is on the wing from March to October, during which time there are two or three broods. Summer broods have slightly darker markings than those that emerge in the spring. Wing markings are similar to those of the Large White, except for two differences: the dark wingtip edging is less extensive on the Small White, and the male has small spots on the top surface of its forewings, unlike those of the Large White which are spotless.

The native population of Small Whites is, in certain years, augmented by large numbers of immigrants from France. This usually occurs in the spring, and the incoming butterflies find feeding grounds by spreading northwards. In late summer a reverse migration takes place when Small Whites head south, back to the Continent. This is not sudden overnight mass emigration. The butterflies move leisurely from one feeding place to another, slowly progressing southwards. I believe that I have evidence of this from my personal butterfly records. Over the last twelve years, between April and September, I have been recording butterfly species and numbers along two rides in West Harling Forest (a section of Thetford Forest) and my records regarding the Small White show a significant surge in the numbers of this butterfly during August each year. If there are just a few Small Whites present, I record the exact number; between five and ten I use the word *'several'*; between ten and fifty *'many'*; between fifty and a hundred *'very many'*; and for greater numbers *'abundant'*. Between the years 1995 and 2000 my records indicate *'many'* or *'very many'* whereas before or after the month of August, I have been regularly recording Small Whites in ones or twos. This strongly suggests the presence of a migratory population feeding for a few days before moving on.

Lifesize

Male

Female

Male.   West Harling Forest, Norfolk
18th June

Female   East Harling, Norfolk
28th August

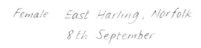

Male.   East Harling, Norfolk
19th August

Female   East Harling, Norfolk
8th September

SMALL WHITE

Pieris rapae

Lifesize

Male

Female

Female in rejection posture
West Harling Forest, Norfolk
5th August

Mating pair
Frosts Common, Norfolk
16th July

Male
East Harling,
Norfolk
16th July

GREEN-VEINED WHITE

Pieris napi

GREEN-VEINED WHITE

The Green-veined White *(Pieris napi)* is found throughout Europe and the British Isles. Populations tend to remain stable, although numbers may be reduced if an unusually dry summer weakens the second brood of the species, causing a depletion of the following year's population. This is a butterfly that thrives best where there is shade and damp grassland with a succession of flowers on which the butterflies can feed, and cruciferous plants such as lady's smock or garlic mustard on which to lay their eggs. *The Millennium Atlas of Butterflies in Britain and Ireland* notes that the Green-veined White was recorded in more 10 kilometre squares than any other species in the 1995–9 survey. In my patch in West Harling Forest, I see Green-veined Whites at almost every visit between April and August. They are double brooded and I have several times photographed mating pairs in May and mid-July. Eggs are laid on garlic mustard and hairy rockcress. In dry places abroad I have seen these butterflies 'mud-puddling' at the edge of woodland streams. Near Brodenbach, on the Mosel in Germany, I watched a mixed group of male and female Green-veined Whites, numbering over thirty individuals, drinking overnight rainwater among a scattering of limestone pebbles. This activity is necessary to replenish body fluids and essential mineral salts lost in mating.

The upperside markings of the Green-veined White, especially those of the second brood, are similar to the markings of the Small White. This can be misleading when trying to identify the butterflies in flight. However, the much heavier underwing vein pattern of *P. napi* gives it a somewhat darker appearance which aids differentiation, although first brood males often appear to be pure white and are usually very small. The 'green' veins which are prominently displayed on the undersurfaces of the wings of the Green-veined White, and give it its name, are due to a distribution of black and yellow scales which, when juxtaposed alongside the veins, appear to be green. The mixing of black and yellow pigments to make a moss-green colour has long been known to artists.

Once, I was able to photograph a male Green-veined White attempting to mate with a female Brimstone butterfly. Presumably he had been attracted by her pale colour and the dark spot on the undersurface of her wing. Despite repeated advances, the Brimstone studiously ignored his attentions. Usually, when a female wishes to reject the advances of a male, she spreads her wings and signals that she has already been impregnated by raising her abdomen at an angle to her thorax, thus making coupling impossible. This rejection pose is shown in the top right picture opposite.

BATH WHITE

During the morning of 4 July 1987, 1 walked upon the walls of Dubrovnik, which surround the old city. The principal buildings were beautiful in the bright sunshine and I spent about an hour photographing the rooftops of the humbler houses, the old tiles of which made interesting compositions of light and shade. Soon the heat became unbearable and I joined my wife who had taken refuge in the shadow of the Old Harbour.

After lunching in the city, we returned to nearby Babin Kuk where we found a small park quite close to our hotel. The shade of trees was inviting and we found seats beneath them. Looking around I noticed several white butterflies flitting around the flowerheads of pink hawksbeard which was growing in a scrubby patch nearby. Thus I had my first sight of Bath White *(Pontia daplidice.)* Fortunately, I had my macro lens with me and, as the butterflies were unconcerned at my near approach, I was able to get several good close-up pictures. It was not until I had the film processed that I realised that all my shots were of female butterflies, as can be seen from the paintings opposite.

Identifying male from female in the Bath White is quite easy when viewing them from above. The dark markings along the edge of the hindwing of the female are not present in the male. Seen from the side, differences are less obvious. The undersurfaces of the hindwings are heavily patterned with dark scales on a yellow ground which (as with the Green-veined White) appears to the eye as green.

Pontia daplidice is distributed in the lands around the western Mediterranean and the islands therein. Further afield, it can be found in the Middle East, Iran and eastwards to Afghanistan and its neighbours. There is a companion species, *Pontia edusa*, which overlaps the range of *P. daplidice*, being present in the eastern Mediterranean, in Greece, the Balkans and Turkey. It is impossible to distinguish between the two species, except in the laboratory following microscopic and biochemical examination. Both species are migratory and, rarely, may be seen in Britain on those infrequent occasions when, as in 1945, there is a mass invasion of the Bath White into the southernmost counties of England.

Why is this butterfly called the Bath White? The history of vernacular names of butterflies is a fascinating study, but I believe that the origin of this particular name is the oddest of all: William Lewin in 1795 illustrated *The Papilios of Great Britain* and included the 'Bath White' stating that the name had been bestowed 'from a piece of needlework executed at Bath by a young lady, from a specimen of this insect, said to have been taken near that place'.

Lifesize

Male

Female

BATH WHITE

Pontia daplidice

Female
Dubrovnik, Croatia
4 th. July

Female
Dubrovnik, Croatia
4 th July

Female
Dubrovnik, Croatia
4 th. July

Lifesize: male

Male
East Harling, Norfolk
9 May

female

Female
West Harling Forest, Norfolk
30 May

Female
West Harling Forest
2 May

Male
Rothley, Northumberland
7 May

ORANGE TIP

Anthocharis cardamines

ORANGE TIP

One of the most handsome symbols of springtime, in my eyes, is the male Orange Tip *(Anthocharis cardamines)*. True, we butterfly watchers are delighted to see the re-emergence of those Brimstone, Comma and Peacock butterflies which have hibernated throughout the winter months, but the smart, fresh appearance of the first male Orange Tips steals the show! The attraction of the male Orange Tip lies in the simplicity of its upper surface wing pattern – a bright splash of orange over nearly half the forewing, with a brown patch at the apex and edged by a black and white fringe. This simple design contrasts sharply with the complex cryptic pattern of the undersides. The orange flash is a warning to a predatory bird that the butterfly tastes dreadful – its body is seasoned with mustard oils passed on from its past life as a caterpillar! Female Orange Tips appear soon after the males, wearing their attractive ensembles of dark grey and white with green-patterned undersides.

This underside colouration provides camouflage, particularly at the end of the day when the butterflies are roosting on white flower heads such as wild candytuft, garlic mustard, rock cress or ribwort plantain. Sometimes, however, they may be in great danger when alighting on white flowerheads because, among the petals, there may be lurking a crab spider lying in wait in the hope of a meal. Once the unsuspecting butterfly is seized in the spider's embrace there is no escape!

When I lived in Northumberland in the early 1980s, the Orange Tip was not often seen, although when one did find these butterflies they tended to be gathered in discrete colonies (sometimes quite numerous), feeding on cuckoo flower. Nowadays, in the Breckland forest, they are usually solitary. I watch the males flying low along the woodland rides, occasionally stopping to feed but soon patrolling onwards in the hope of finding a mate. When they are successful, a few brief courtship manoeuvres take place before coupling. On 12 April 2000, I photographed a male Orange Tip being rejected by a female, using the usual rejection signal by raising her abdomen until it was almost at right-angles to her thorax to indicate that she was already gravid, even at this early date. This, perhaps, is an illustration of the priority and urgency they ascribe to procreation in order to preserve the species.

Eggs are laid on a variety of crucifers but I have noticed that, in West Harling Forest near where I live, female Orange Tips seem to be very particular in choosing their host plant. Large clumps of garlic mustard are to be found in parts of the forest and yet the females will spend much time seeking out isolated single plants of hairy rockcress on which to lay their eggs. I wonder why?

CLOUDED YELLOW

Of the three species of Clouded Yellow that have been recorded in Britain – the Pale Clouded Yellow *(Colias hyale)*, Berger's Clouded Yellow *(Colias alfacanensis)*, and the Clouded Yellow *(Colias croceus)*, the latter is the one most likely to be seen in my part of the country, Breckland. The Clouded Yellow breeds freely and may have up to four broods a year in its native Mediterranean stronghold. In those years when its numbers outstrip its local food supply (principally clovers, lucerne and trefoils) the butterflies migrate northwards in the spring and settle throughout northern Europe, including Britain and southern Ireland. Large-scale migration does not occur every year. In 1983, when an outstanding invasion brought waves of Clouded Yellows to settle in nearly all counties of England and Wales, local breeding populations were established during August and September. Few, if any, survived the winter because at no stage of their development are they adapted for hibernation.

It was in 1983 when I first saw a Clouded Yellow. On 4 August, on wasteland near Leeds, I was able to approach within a metre of a male resting on birdsfoot trefoil leaves. On 29 September I was able to obtain excellent photographs of a female on a disused railway embankment near Newcastle airport and, a day or two later, I got more close-up pictures at a park in Teignmouth in Devon. In later years I have been able to photograph Clouded Yellows in Slovenia, Croatia and Italy, but it has been at nearby West Harling Forest and at Redgrave and Lopham Fen that I have had the chance of watching their behaviour in detail. I have noticed the aggressiveness of the males, which repeatedly leave their nectaring to attack other males. They are very restless and difficult to approach, unlike the females, which are much more passive. Often I find that the easiest way to differentiate between the sexes is by watching their behaviour.

Clouded Yellows, when settled, usually have their wings closed. Their sex can then best be determined by carefully looking at the trailing edges of the closed wings. Given good light it is possible to see the yellow patches, which break up the dark wing borders in the female, showing through the underside of the wings. This can be seen in the lower left painting, which illustrates the Clouded Yellow *Colias croceus helice*, a female form that occurs in about 10 per cent of the population.

From time to time I am asked to lead small groups of interested people around my 'patch' in the forest. On 19 July 1992, when leading a party from the Thetford Natural History Society, I happened to be the first person to spot a distant Clouded Yellow. When I pointed this out, some of the group were quite thrilled and congratulated me. Some five years later, in August 1997, leading the same group of people, I again noticed a solitary Clouded Yellow before anyone else but this time, far from being congratulated, I was accused of carrying around a Clouded Yellow in a box and releasing it when no one was looking!

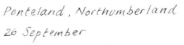

Female
Ponteland, Northumberland
26 September

Male, lifesize

Female, lifesize

Male
Redgrave & Lopham Fen
Norfolk
25 August

Female, form helice
West Harling Forest
5 August

CLOUDED YELLOW

Colias croceus

Male, lifesize

Female, lifesize

Female
East Harling, Norfolk
5th May

Pair resting after courtship flight
West Harling Forest, 12th May

Male
West Harling Forest
12th September

BRIMSTONE

Gonepteryx rhamni

BRIMSTONE

The distribution map of the Brimstone butterfly *(Gonepteryx rhamni)* in *The Millennium Atlas of Butterflies in Britain and Ireland* shows that, north of Yorkshire, the butterfly is represented by only single sightings. This explains why, when I lived in Northumberland, I had to travel westwards to Grizedale Forest in the Lake District to obtain my first photograph of a Brimstone. Since moving to Breckland, I find that I now have almost a hundred slides depicting Brimstones. Why have I become so obsessed with this insect? Well, partly because it is so often seen in and around our local forest, and the temptation to get yet another shot is often irresistible; partly because it has a beautiful shape and is not at all camera-shy; but chiefly as a result of my deep interest in its life-cycle, especially its courtship behaviour.

The Brimstone is long-lived, being present either on the wing or in hibernation for almost a year. It has few design faults. Although it lacks any cryptic pattern to confuse a potential predator, it is provided with excellent camouflage when it simulates a leaf (veins and all) when roosting or hibernating. Its long proboscis allows it to feed on a wide range of flowers, and its caterpillar food plants, purging buckthorn or alder buckthorn, are usually plentiful in its breeding areas.

When male Brimstones awake from their hibernation (in late March, hereabout) they seek nectar from dandelions, primroses or ground ivy to replenish their energy reserve. Females appear a few weeks later and for a few days show no interest in the males. Indeed, it is quite usual to see males and females feeding side by side on the same clump of dandelions. But this soon changes as hormones rise, and, by the first week in May, courtship display is noted and females may be observed laying their single, pale-green eggs on the young leaves of buckthorn.

My observations suggest that scent and taste play a big part in Brimstone courtship. Usually there is a spiralling courtship flight during which wing movements assist the distribution of pheromones or aphrodisiacs. Sometimes the female is leading the flight, sometimes the male. Eventually they flop down beside each other, the female with her wings wide open. Then the male walks over her outstretched wings, perhaps testing her quality as a prospective mate through the taste organs on his feet. He may then caress her with his antennae. This foreplay may last for several minutes before the pair rise in the air together. Presumably, they couple shortly afterwards, though despite my having several photographs of their earlier courtship manoeuvres, I have never seen Brimstones coupled. An episode in their courtship is illustrated opposite.

WOOD WHITE

On 7 July 1989, during a bright summer morning, I watched several Wood White *(Leptidea sinapis)* butterflies flying low over a grassy clearing in the State Forest above Brodenbach on the Mosel in Germany. There were other butterflies about, but the Wood Whites were distinctive because of their comparatively small size and weak, jinking flight which seemed to be without purpose or direction. Occasionally, one would settle to feed at a flower and I would attempt to get near enough to photograph it but, despite its apparent frailty, it quickly reacted to my approach and fluttered away. I followed a number of these butterflies hoping to get a reasonably close-up shot, but to no avail. After nearly an hour's effort, my only reward was a rather distant picture of a Wood White perched on the flower of greater birdsfoot trefoil.

I have tried to find the Wood White in England, twice visiting woods which they are known to colonise, but each time I have failed to find a single one; even a visit to Salcey Forest (a well-known stronghold of the Wood White) had to be aborted due to heavy rain. I have had the best opportunities of studying and photographing the Wood White in Austria and Slovenia and, more recently, in the Spanish Pyrenees where I saw several groups 'mud-puddling' at the edges of streams. Presumably these were males, augmenting their diet with mineral salts contained in the mud.

The upper surfaces of the Wood White are a pure white, with a dark patch at the tip of the forewing and a scattering of dark scales along the leading edge. The undersides of the hindwings, which are more often seen as the butterfly rests with its wings closed, have patches of dark scales which produce a vague pattern of varied intensity. In continental Wood Whites, which have two broods, the first brood has darker underwings than those of the second brood. The amount of light cast upon their wings can also affect their apparent colour and, when seen in flight, they appear to be much whiter than when seen resting.

This species is fairly common in Ireland, but in England it is confined to the counties of Hereford, Worcestershire, Northamptonshire, Oxfordshire, the wooded area between Surrey and Sussex, and a few areas of undercliff between Sidmouth and Lyme Regis. In woodland, continuing survival of the Wood White depends upon appropriate management, particularly ensuring the right amount of shade to encourage tall growth of the vetches *(Lathyrus* species) on which most Wood White eggs are laid.

Lifesize

Male

Female

Female
Bohinj, Slovenia
1st July

Female
Kirchberg, Austria
27th June

Male
Bohinj
1st July

Male
Brodenbach/Mosel, Germany
early July

WOOD WHITE

Leptidea sinapis

3
Lycaenidae:

HAIRSTREAKS, COPPERS & BLUES

PURPLE HAIRSTREAK

WHITE-LETTER HAIRSTREAK

GREEN HAIRSTREAK

SMALL COPPER

HOLLY BLUE

SMALL BLUE

SILVER-STUDDED BLUE

BROWN ARGUS

CASTLE EDEN ARGUS

MAZARINE BLUE

CHALK-HILL BLUE

ADONIS BLUE

COMMON BLUE

DUKE OF BURGUNDY

PURPLE HAIRSTREAK

I think that I must have been very lucky in my first attempt to photograph the Purple Hairstreak *(Quercusia quercus)*. The presence of these butterflies in the neighbourhood was reported to me by a friend who, while carrying out a traffic survey on a public road running through the Duke of Grafton's estate near Euston on the Norfolk/Suffolk border, had observed Purple Hairstreaks flitting among the high branches of roadside oak trees. On 1 August 1989, I parked my car at this place and soon spotted the Hairstreaks. After briefly scanning the treetops with binoculars, I noticed that one butterfly had descended onto a patch of nettles nearby. Taking care not to cast my shadow on it, I slowly advanced until I had the butterfly almost filling the viewfinder. Its wings were spread, but why weren't they purple? I held my breath as it shifted its position slightly and there appeared a lovely gleam of purple on two segments of each forewing. Slowly I pressed the firing button and had captured on film a lovely female Purple Hairstreak! (see the centre left painting).

Two years later, I got even better pictures. In late July at a small nature reserve at Brettenham Heath, which lies on Peddar's Way beside the Norwich to Thetford main road, I spotted a Purple Hairstreak feeding on the flowers of wild parsnip. I got a nice picture of the underside wing pattern of what I believe was a female. I returned to Brettenham Heath on two successive days and obtained more close-up shots. These formed the basis for the other paintings reproduced opposite.

I have read some accounts questioning the extent to which the Purple Hairstreak will feed from flowers or come to ground level to sip aphid honeydew, the main source of food obtained on high from the oak leaves. For what they are worth, here are a few observations I recorded on slides during 1989: a female feeding on ragwort; a worn male feeding on hemp agrimony; a female sipping honeydew on a bramble leaf in Germany.

The colouration and markings of the Purple Hairstreak may be studied in the paintings. I was very interested to read in *Butterflies of Great Britain & Ireland* that those eminent writers A. Maitland Emmet and John Heath described the forewing colour of the Purple Hairstreak as 'deep purplish fuscous irrorate submetallic indigo blue'. I have no doubt that they are perfectly correct. As a mere artist, I would settle for purplish blue or ultramarine with a dash of crimson lake!

Lifesize

Male

Female

Male.
Brettenham Heath, Norfolk
1st. August

Female. Rushfordroad Belts, Norfolk
1st. August

Female. Brettenham Heath
30th July

Male. Brettenham Heath
1st August

PURPLE HAIRSTREAK

Quercusia quercus

Lifesize

Male

Female

Female
West Harling Forest, Norfolk
22nd July

Male
West Harling Forest
5th August

Male
West Harling Forest
24th July

WHITE-LETTER HAIRSTREAK

Strymonidia w-album

WHITE-LETTER HAIRSTREAK

The name 'White-letter Hairstreak' is obviously descriptive of the underwing pattern of this butterfly, which clearly displays a bright letter 'W' when its wings are closed. A similar splash of white is to be found on all Hairstreaks and is presumably intended to startle or confuse a potential predator. Similarly, most Hairstreaks bear small 'tails' on the lower trailing edge of the hindwing which, in conjunction with an eye spot, form part of their 'back-to-front' mimicry.

The White-letter Hairstreak butterfly *(Strymonidia w-album)*, like the Purple Hairstreak, spends much of its adult life standing on leaves high up its host tree. When the sun shines and the aphid honeydew is plentiful, these butterflies pad around the upper surface of the leaves tasting the sweet substance with their feet and dabbing it with their proboscides to suck up the energy-supplying syrup of honeydew. Both these species overwinter as eggs; indeed, they spend almost three-quarters of their life-cycle in that state, although for much of that time the egg contains a perfectly-formed tiny caterpillar. Eggs of the White-letter Hairstreak are usually laid on elm twigs, just below flower buds, the female choosing a sheltered twig and on its sunny side. In the forest near my home, the host plant is invariably the smooth-leaved elm which is common in East Anglia.

The White-letter Hairstreak is extremely difficult to find on my patch. I have searched for it over ten years and have found it at only two locations: one a long-established site, appropriately named Elm Bank; the other on a forest ride about a kilometre from Elm Bank. My sightings have been few, the first taking place at Elm Bank on 19 July 1997 when I spotted a splendid, fresh-looking female feeding on creeping thistle. Nine days later, I found a rather faded specimen on the same thistlehead. On 5 August the following year at the second site, I saw a very scruffy male feeding on ragwort. I searched for elm at this site, eventually finding a solitary, weak-looking elm sapling wedged between oaks and conifers. A visit to the same site the following year yielded nothing. On 24 July 1999, I was more successful when I spotted a perfect male on ragwort. This one allowed me to take six close-up photographs of him! My paintings are somewhat tidied-up versions of what I caught on film.

GREEN HAIRSTREAK

I think that the Green Hairstreak *(Callophrys rubi)* is a little gem of a butterfly! In late April or early May when I first spot one (usually a male) perched just above eye-level on a hawthorn bush, I thrill at the sight. Sometimes, so great is my joy that I have been known to stop a passing dog-walker to point out this splendid insect. Invariably, he or she will share my excitement, usually because they didn't know that there was such a thing as a bright green butterfly!

In the North of England, at Dipton Wood near Hexham in Northumberland, I have had the pleasure of observing a large colony of Green Hairstreak butterflies and being able to compare them with the activities of the same species in south Norfolk where I live now.

Dipton Wood stands on acid heathland. In early May 1984 I made the first of several visits to a large clearing in the wood around which were stands of silver birch trees and a few gorse bushes. Covering the ground layer of the clearing were many shrubs of bilberry, and among the leaves of those shrubs were about a hundred Green Hairstreaks! They were feeding on the bilberry flowers, mating and laying eggs on the leaf shoots. Almost all of them were active at a height of less than 1 metre, which meant that I had to kneel to photograph them. Because these insects are not secretive like the Hairstreaks that live on treetops, I was able to take over twenty intimate pictures of them. Comparing these pictures with the sixty or so that I have subsequently taken in the South, one can see that whereas almost all of the Dipton Wood specimens are of the form *punctata* with well-marked white streaks on the underside of both wings, most of the Green Hairstreak photographs taken in Breckland have scarcely any white markings; indeed many are form *caecus*, entirely without hairstreaks.

During my time in Breckland, over about fifteen years, I have only once seen a collection of Green Hairstreaks which could be called a colony. This was on 4 May 1999 when among many broom bushes in West Harling Forest at a place appropriately called Broom Covert, I recorded seeing about thirty Green Hairstreaks. These butterflies were all on the broom flowers and stems and consequently were more or less at eye-level, making photography easy. At about the same date in May in 2000 and 2001 I stood in the same place with the air laden with pollen from the masses of broom flowers, but failed to find a single Green Hairstreak! Over the years, I have noticed these fluctuations in the numbers of Green Hairstreaks along the rides that I patrol. The flowers of gorse and broom appear on time, but there are few, if any, butterflies. I used to ascribe these deficits in local *rubi* populations to particularly wet winters, but as it is now believed that the Green Hairstreak chrysalis spends the winter deep in an ants' nest, I must look elsewhere for an explanation of the fluctuations in Green Hairstreak numbers.

Lifesize

West Harling Forest, Norfolk
27th May

Male

Female

Mating pair
Dipton Wood, Northumberland
4th June

GREEN HAIRSTREAK

Callophrys rubi

Dipton Wood,
Northumberland
1st June

Lifesize

Bolam Lake, Northumberland
3rd October

West Harling Forest, Norfolk
25th May

f. caeruleopunctata Rühl

West Harling Forest, Norfolk
27th July

f. caeruleopunctata Rühl
West Harling Forest, Norfolk
16th May

SMALL COPPER

Lycaena phlaeas

SMALL COPPER

This little jewel of a butterfly is seen throughout the butterfly 'season' between May and October. There are two main generations and often a third, smaller one. The spring brood flies between May and June; the second between July and August; and the autumn brood from September to mid-October. The third brood is not necessarily confined to southern counties, as I have photographed the Small Copper *(Lycaena phlaens)* in Northumberland in mid-October.

Some years see the development of quite large colonies, like the one I recorded on 10 August 1998 at Brettenham Heath, near Thetford, where I estimated that well over fifty Small Coppers were occupying a site of about one-eighth of an acre. Earlier records in my logbook show 'over forty' on 26 May 1987 in West Harling Forest, and 'about fifty' at West Stow Country Park in Suffolk some four days later. On most occasions when walking my usual transect in the forest, my count of the Small Copper will be just one or two.

Male Small Coppers defend their territories pugnaciously. I well remember warning a group of naturalists I was taking around my 'patch' in West Harling Forest that when we reached a certain point on the ride we would see, and probably be attacked by, a solitary male Small Copper. Sure enough, precisely on cue, he rose and circled our party several times until we had walked on. Once, when visiting a certain place in the forest, hoping to find a White-letter Hairstreak, I sat for over an hour watching a clump of creeping thistle on which a Small Copper was standing guard. He stayed there during the whole of my time there, and was sitting on the same flower head when I returned the following day. I can only assume that the passing female for which he was waiting had jilted him!

The colouring and wing patterns of the Small Copper are exquisite. When the butterfly is seen with opened wings, obliquely from above, and the sunlight catches the forewing where it joins the thorax, one can see a beautiful, golden, metallic sheen at the wing root. Another attractive feature of the wings is in the form *caeruleopunctata* where the orange markings along the trailing edge of the hindwing are augmented by an inner row of cobalt blue spots. This form is illustrated in the two lower paintings.

I have witnessed the courtship of the Small Copper only once, and that briefly. I was sitting at the edge of a forest clearing somewhere in Coquetdale among the Northumbrian hills. Nearby was a rustic picnic table on which were standing two Small Copper butterflies facing each other a few centimetres apart. It is very difficult to tell the male from the female in this species but one of the butterflies, probably the male, had his wings wide open and was shaking them rapidly as if he were trembling. Perhaps he was distributing pheromones from the androconia (specialised scent scales) on his wings. After a few seconds the two butterflies took off together and, following a brief twisting flight, they dropped into the long grass, probably to mate.

HOLLY BLUE

Throughout the years I have lived in Norfolk, I have been fortunate in having had breeding Holly Blues *(Celastrina argiolus)* in my garden almost every year. Being so close at hand I have been able to study and photograph them in some detail, especially the development of the caterpillars and their association with black garden ants. The female Holly Blue lays her eggs at the base of flower buds on the female holly tree; on the young, sprouting leaves of the male holly; and, in my garden, sometimes on the immature berries of firethorn.

When the larvae are very small they appear to be disregarded by patrolling ants, but as they develop they are regularly attended by ants. The ants merely attend a larva, and make no attempt to divert it or influence its progress when it moves around the host plant. Usually, one or two ants act as outriders, while one or two others show interest in the caterpillar's seventh segment where a special gland is situated. This is called 'Newcomer's gland', and it is seen as a small, transverse invagination which can be stimulated to secrete a kind of 'honeydew' on which the ants feed. Sometimes ants are seen to use their antennae to drum around the gland and cause it to open and secrete. In addition to Newcomer's gland on the seventh segment, two dorso-lateral organs or tubercles on each side of the eighth segment of the larva also have some significance for ants. On one occasion I saw these two tubercles being suddenly erected, causing immediate excitement on the part of two nearby ants. The tubercles were soon retracted. I have no idea what this meant.

The Holly Blue larva is not giving the ants a 'free lunch' however: in return, the larvae expect to receive protection. I had proof of this protection being given on 17 June 1993. On that day I was watching a Holly Blue caterpillar on a 'walkabout' looking for immature berries elsewhere on the tree. As it ascended the stem, escorted by five ants, a spider made a sudden attack. In a split second it was thwarted by the rapid reaction of one of the ants. The spider appeared to be momentarily paralysed, before scuttling off to hide among the leaves. I assume that it must have been sprayed with formic acid by the defending ant. I was lucky to be able to photograph this event.

The Holly Blue butterfly is double brooded, the first generation appearing from mid-April to June, the second emerging in mid-July to August. In most cases the second brood females lay their eggs on ivy, although other host plants are used. Like the Green Hairstreak, the Holly Blue is not shy and can often be approached closely. The butterfly prefers to feed on leaves coated with aphid honeydew rather than take nectar from flowers; thus it is often seen among bushes and trees. Its handsome appearance can be judged from the paintings opposite.

Egg-laying female
on firethorn buds
East Harling,
Norfolk
14 May

Lifesize

Male

Female
(summer brood)

Female
East Harling
22 May

Male
East Harling, 26 April

Male
East Harling, 26 April

HOLLY BLUE

Celastrina argiolus

Lifesize

Male

Female

Male.
St. Abbs, Scotland
late May

Male. Compton Down, Isle of Wight
20 July

Female. St Abbs, Scotland
late May

SMALL OR LITTLE BLUE

Cupido minimus

SMALL BLUE

The Small or Little Blue *(Cupido minimus)* as its specific name implies is the smallest British butterfly, being about the size of an adult thumbnail. It is widespread throughout Continental Europe and the lands surrounding the Baltic. In Britain there may be two generations a year in the South, but usually May to the end of June is the time when the butterfly may be found in the North of Britain. It lives in small colonies in most parts, widely distributed from John O' Groats to Portland Bill. They are usually confined to traditional sites in sunny ravines, disused quarries and embankments where the larval food plant, kidney vetch, flourishes.

In late May 1982 my friend Peter West and I, with our wives, drove from our home village near Newcastle-upon-Tyne up into Scotland to find a Small Blue colony at Coldingham Bay near St Abbs. The site was on the south-facing side of a ravine leading down to the sea. Long ago this would probably have been a river estuary. The weather was windy and dull, and we wondered whether we would be able to find these tiny insects. None were flying, but a closer inspection of the rough hillside revealed several Small Blues among the litter of dead grasses and bright new growth. Kidney vetch was growing in strong clumps. I was able to get ten good photographs. One picture shows a female sipping nectar from a dandelion; all the rest show males or females sheltering from the wind and perched low down on grass stems or blades. The male that I have illustrated middle right in the paintings opposite shows an usually large area of blue scales on his forewing upper surfaces.

At the other end of Britain on the Isle of Wight, I have several times found Small Blues at the edge of a small car park beside the A3055 near Compton Down. Again, this is a south-facing hillside. In Italy, halfway up Monte Baldo above Malcesine on Lake Garda, I found a colony of the Small Blue, this time feeding among orange-flowered kidney vetch.

It is interesting to note that, like the Holly Blue and other blue butterflies, the Small Blue has an affinity with ants, through which the ants may give protection to the larvae and pupae of this butterfly when they are overwintering.

SILVER-STUDDED BLUE

I cannot claim to have had a wide experience of the Silver-studded Blue *(Plebejus argus)*; indeed it was not until 1988 that I first set eyes on one. On 17 July of that year, I visited Horsford Woods, north of Norwich, and spent a happy morning walking about the large patch of residual heathland still preserved there, enjoying the sight of many Silver-studded Blue butterflies and taking about a dozen photographs of them. This site is in the Wensum Forest area which comprises the old heaths around Horsford, Buxton and Marsham. The area sustains a complex of *argus* colonies which, though not comparable with the huge populations of some of the heathlands in southern England and the North Wales coastal colonies, continue to survive in good numbers, though their numbers fluctuate year by year. In Horsford Woods the caterpillars feed on the tender stems of ling, bell heather, cross-leaved heath and gorse. As we saw with the Holly Blue, the larvae of the Silver-studded Blue have a close relationship with ants. Research has shown that the female butterfly chooses to lay her eggs in the vicinity of ant populations.

The Silver-studded Blue is single brooded and the butterflies can be seen on the wing from July to August, but some colonies in Suffolk and North Wales emerge some weeks earlier. Like the emergence pattern of most butterfly species, males appear before females and, as the life expectancy of the Silver-studded Blues averages only about four days, mating takes place soon after the female emerges.

In *The Butterflies of Britain & Ireland* Jeremy Thomas writes that his brother Chris observed a newly emerged Silver-studded Blue being guarded by a group of ants whilst undertaking the task of inflating its wings, a time when it is very vulnerable to attack by a predator. Futhermore, the ants had probably been attracted to the butterfly by the presence of the natal fluid coating its body! This is yet another example of the apparent bond between ant and butterfly – well, perhaps not a bond, more a marriage of convenience!

For some time, I have been concerned that the photographs I took of the male Silver-studded Blue at Horsford Woods show the upper wing surfaces to be of a colour much at variance to the colour shown in many field guide illustrations. I was unaware of the variation of colour and pattern which can occur in this species. The painting of the male (centre right, opposite) shows wings of a greyish blue, not the purplish blue of the textbooks and field guides. What I have photographed and subsequently painted appears to be the aberration *plumbeus,* and I believe that all the males I saw at Horsford were this colour. Furthermore, when in the Spanish Pyrenees in late June 2001, I photographed several Silver-studded Blues of the same upper wing colour. Perhaps specimens of *plumbeus* gave rise to the early names for *Plebejus argus* – e.g. Small Lead Argus (Petiver 1717) and Lead Blue (Rennie 1832).

SILVER-STUDDED BLUE

Plebejus argus

Male.
Horsford Woods. Norfolk
17th July

Lifesize

Male

Female

Male
Horsford Woods
17th July

Female.
Horsford Woods
17th July

Female. Horsford Woods. 17th July

Female, lifesize

Female
West Harling Forest, Norfolk
31 May

Newly-emerged male,
West Harling Forest
27 May

Male
West Harling Forest
31 May

Male
West Harling Forest
31 May

BROWN ARGUS

Aricia agestis

BROWN ARGUS

I began recording butterflies on 1 June 1983 at the age of fifty-nine (Oh! those wasted years) when I lived in Northumberland, but I had to wait until I moved south before I saw a Brown Argus *(Aricia agestis)*. In June 1986 I started making regular visits to certain rides in West Harling Forest, an area which I soon came to regard as my 'patch'. Even then, it was not until 31 May 1987 that I was able to write in my logbook: 'Brown Argus 50+ newly emerged'. The following year on 28 May, I noted: 'Brown Argus several 100s newly emerged – noted a bluish patina on bodies and wings – very active – some attempting to mate'. Now, it is well known that the Brown Argus doesn't have any blue colouring, but some of these fresh specimens certainly had a bluish sheen. A few days later, most of this large congregation of butterflies had vanished. Successive years produced more modest numbers.

My most regular observations of Brown Argus in the forest took place on a ride which underwent several changes. Some breeding sites became shaded out by the rapid growth of the young pine plantings; some were abandoned owing to the spread of bracken; others became overgrown as the rabbits disappeared. Nevertheless, the ride, with its wide grassy edges and abundance of wild flowers, remains a good place for butterflies.

We are inclined to blame farmers, builders, planners, road makers and even forestry managers for the loss of butterfly habitat. I must now confess my guilt in completely destroying the breeding ground of a small colony of Brown Argus butterflies *in my garden!* In the early 1990s, I began sending records of the butterflies in my garden to Dr Margaret Vickery, who collects records of garden butterflies for Butterfly Conservation. On 26 July 1995, I recorded a Brown Argus in my garden, and during successive days noted these butterflies nectaring on potentilla, reflex stonecrop and knapweed flowers in the back garden. Usually, these were just single butterflies. The following year their presence became more commonplace and on 8 August I noted three in the garden at the same time. Eight days later, in the early evening of 16 August I was delighted to find eleven Brown Arguses roosting on my lavender hedge in the front garden! They were still sleeping there early the following morning, but had flown by eight o'clock. Knowing that the Brown Argus is a fairly sedentary species that travel no more than 180 metres from their birthplace, and knowing that my house is surrounded by other houses, I began to wonder if this was my own special colony. My front lawn was not so much a lawn, more a plot of British weeds. It was really quite a mess. So, during that winter I had it dug up and replaced the grass with shingle. Since that time, I haven't seen a single Brown Argus in the garden. I feel very sad that I cannot continue sending Dr Vickery reports of Brown Argus, especially when I recall that in 1996, mine was one of only fourteen records reporting this butterfly in their gardens.

I hope that my paintings will give some indication of the beautiful creature I turned away from my doorstep!

CASTLE EDEN ARGUS /
NORTHERN BROWN ARGUS

I have not been accurate in naming this butterfly. I have called it Castle Eden Argus, a vernacular name, but not now officially recognised. These butterflies used to be prized by collectors, who labelled them Castle Eden Dene Argus, and they were regarded as a subspecies of the Northern Brown Argus *(Aricia artaxerxes)*. Now they are shown to be merely a form of the Northern Brown Argus, and should be named *Aricia artaxerxes f. salmacis*.

Superficially these butterflies closely resemble the Brown Argus but genetically they are closer to the Northern Brown Argus of the Continent. Unlike the Brown Argus, which has two broods a year, *artaxerxes* has only one. This is not due to their more northern environment, but to their genetic make-up.

The Northern Brown Argus is found in Scotland and northern England. It is confined to thinly scattered, isolated colonies. Some of these colonies have existed for centuries in the same location (the Eden Dene butterflies still breed on the same locations, on either side of the estuary, as they did in 1827). Indeed, the Northern Brown Argus is thought to have been one the earliest butterflies to re-colonise Britain when warmer conditions developed after the last Ice Age. Today its range includes many alpine sites and lands as far north as Finland and northern Norway.

The most notable distinguishing feature of the British *artaxerxes*, a feature which attracted collectors, is a white discoidal spot on the upper forewings which stands out against the deep brown of the wings' ground colour. Other features include an absence, or near absence, of orange lunules on the upperside of the forewings of the male, and the white discs which pattern the undersides of the wings of both sexes display only small black centre spots, or lack them altogether. The form *salmacis* at Castle Eden Dene, generally speaking, do not display these *artaxerxes* features – the white upperwing disc is replaced by a black one (with or without a white halo around it) and the underwing white discs contain prominent black spots. These features may be seen in the paintings.

On 27 July 1980, my friend Peter West and I arrived at the estuary of the River Eden. This lies near the colliery village of Horden, just south of the town of Peterlee, County Durham. It was a beautiful, sunny day. The estuary is flanked by hummocky, grassy cliffs bedecked with wild flowers. We chose to explore the northern, south-facing cliff and soon spotted the *salmacis* butterflies. They allowed us to approach close, and I was able to take eight pictures, some showing the butterflies on common rock-rose and hop trefoil. The rock-rose is the usual host plant on which eggs are laid, and on which the *salmacis* caterpillars feed. Although I didn't realise it at the time, all my shots were of females which was disappointing, as I had hoped to record both sexes.

Male

Female

Female
Castle Eden Dene
27th July

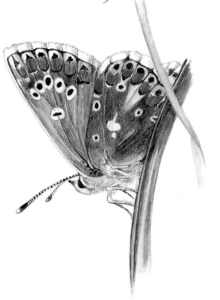

Female
Castle Eden Dene, Co. Durham
27th July

CASTLE EDEN ARGUS

Aricia artaxerxes salmacis

Female, Castle Eden Dene, 27th July

Female
Castle Eden Dene
27th July

Male
Salzkammergut, Austria
29 June

Female
Salzkammergut,
Austria
26 June

Lifesize

Male

Female

MAZARINE BLUE

Cyaniris semiargus

Male
Tirol, Austria
27 June

Female, Spanish Pyrenees, 18 June

MAZARINE BLUE

In June 1983, my wife and I had a motoring holiday in the Salzkammergut region of Austria. We had decided to divide our time between butterfly hunting and visiting the cities of Salzburg and Vienna. During the first week of our holiday we found a beautiful, flower-filled meadow through which a babbling stream meandered, providing 'background music' to our butterfly watching. There was a splendid variety of butterflies to be seen, several previously unknown to me, and among them we found our first Mazarine Blues *(Cyaniris semiargus)*. I was particularly happy to find this butterfly, having read that it had once fluttered around English meadows, albeit in small numbers. I was able to photograph a female laying an egg on red clover, with her abdomen buried deep in the flowerhead. Most of the females were feeding on clover; the few males we spotted were basking on grass.

Three years later, in late June 1986, we renewed our acquaintance with the Mazarine Blue in the Austrian Tirol and, more recently, I was able to record them on six successive days at various places in the Spanish Pyrenees.

In Britain the Mazarine Blue has always been scarce. Indeed, doubts have been expressed that it was ever really established here – rather, that its infrequent appearances were the result of migration from the Continent where it has always been widespread. However, it is now recognised that the records of the almost continuous presence, between 1808 and 1841, of a colony near Glanvilles Wootton, south of Sherborne in Dorset, constituted an established colony. These records were contained in the journal of J.C. Dale who lived nearby. There may also have been a colony in the Cardiff area as twelve Mazarine Blues were caught there in 1876. The Mazarine Blue has been recorded in twenty-two English counties since 1710, mostly in the South, but there is no means of being certain how many were the result of sporadic migration, or were stray vagrants.

Butterfly collectors, despairing of obtaining British specimens, turned to buying them from dealers on the Continent. A.M. Stewart, writing in 1918 in his book *British Butterflies* about the Mazarine Blue suggests: 'Good continental specimens can be purchased cheaply. And I hold it better to fill your row with these, carefully labelling their source, than to have empty spaces always staring you in the face. Unless the species becomes more common, the average collector's chance of capturing British specimens is extremely remote'.

The Mazarine Blue has only one brood a year throughout most of Europe. Its flight period may be at any time between May and October, depending upon altitude and location. The larval food plant is almost invariably red clover. My paintings illustrate the marked difference between the colour of the upper wing surfaces in the male and female. This makes identification easy when the butterflies have their wings open, although when their wings are closed sex differentiation is more difficult.

CHALK-HILL BLUE

From my home in south Norfolk, the nearest place where I can find the Chalk-hill Blue *(Lysandra coridon)* is along the Devil's Dyke on the edge of Newmarket Heath and just within the Cambridgeshire border. This site is at the northern limit of the Chalk-hill Blue's main breeding counties. I have not visited it, but my friends report having seen large numbers there. Most of my watching has taken place on the South Downs, near Lewes, and on the Isle of Wight at Compton Down, Mottestone Down and at a disused chalkpit near Brightstone Down. This last place was an ideal spot to get really close to the Chalk-hill Blue. Stalking butterflies on the wide expanse of downland can be frustrating as they have adequate warning of one's approach and ample space to fly off to a more distant clump of flowers on which to feed. Within the smaller confines of a chalkpit they have less inclination to move on.

The old workings in the chalkpit had left the ground uneven and the little hills and dells, long grassed-over and grazed by rabbits, were covered with wild flowers. Horseshoe vetch and marjoram were very much in evidence. I took most of my photographs at close quarters, the butterflies being so intent on sipping nectar from the flowers that my presence was ignored. This took place on 27 July 1988. I revisited the chalkpit on 27 May 1992 when I spotted Adonis Blues. I followed one down a chalky slope, caught my foot in a rabbit burrow, and sprained my ankle. I spent the rest of the short holiday hobbling about with a walking stick! On a later visit in May 2000, I discovered that this splendid butterfly site had been used as a motorbike rough riding track and was closed by a barbed-wire barrier.

The Chalk-hill Blue has four requirements in its habitat: chalk downland (or limestone hills); the caterpillar food plant horseshoe vetch; a warm sunny aspect; and the security afforded by attendant ants. This mutually beneficial association with ants plays an important part in the butterfly's life-cycle, especially during its larval stage.

The male Chalk-hill Blue is easily identified: its upper surfaces are a delightful powder blue, gradually darkening to become a black border at the outer edge of the wing, and then framed by a white fringe, crossed by narrow, dark lines. The male's ground colour is a much paler blue than any other Blue butterfly in Britain. The underside wing surfaces, though heavily patterned, also have a pale ground colour and sometimes appear almost white. In contrast, the female is altogether darker and difficult to differentiate, especially on her underside, from the Adonis and Common Blue females. Perhaps the easiest way to distinguish the female is when she is in a colony with males. Identify the males and assume that their partners belong to the same species!

Male.
Compton Down, Isle of Wight
27 July

Lifesize

Male

Female

CHALK-HILL BLUE

Lysandra coridon

Male
Compton Down
20 July

Female
Brightstone, I.O.W.
27 July

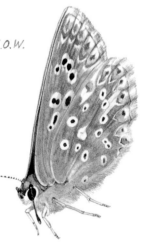

Female. Brightstone
27 July

Male. Ranmore Common Surrey
18th August

Male

Female

Female, Ranmore Common
24th August

Female. Ranmore Common
18th August

Male
Ranmore Common
18th August

ADONIS BLUE

Lysandra bellargus

ADONIS BLUE

When I was butterfly watching in Northumberland, the largest number of species I could expect to record during a butterfly walk was a modest nine. So, in the hope of finding more butterflies, in late June 1984 my wife and I took a holiday in Slovenia, in what was then a unified Yugoslavia. We stayed on the shore of Lake Bohinj in the Julian Alps and, during a fortnight, we recorded forty-one species. It was here that I saw my first Adonis Blue *(Lysandra bellargus)*. I clearly remember being struck by the intensity of the blue on the wings of a male. The cobalt blue is almost metallic and I noticed that it could reflect nearby colours, giving the wings a greenish tint when it settled in grassland. During the day that I took my first photograph of an Adonis Blue, I was also blessed with the opportunity of getting close pictures of a mating pair, using a slab of limestone as their nuptial bed!

In Britain, the Adonis Blue is at the northern limit of its range and therefore is clustered in the southernmost counties of England wherever there is chalk grassland, a warm local climate, an abundance of its larval food plant horseshoe vetch, and guardian ants. These requirements exactly match those of its congener the Chalk-hill Blue. The Adonis Blue has one further requirement however: it must have well-grazed grass less than 5 centimetres high, thus restricting the breeding sites. In this respect the Adonis Blue is more choosy than the Chalk-hill Blue which may utilise sites abandoned by the Adonis Blue. Unlike the Chalk-hill Blue however, which has only one brood a year, the Adonis Blue has two, and may be seen flying from mid-May to June, and August to mid-September. The Adonis Blue associates with ants perhaps even more so than the Chalk-hill Blue.

On 18 August 1991, Joan and I visited Ranmore Common, near Dorking. We planned to have a day of shared interests: I was to spend the morning scrambling all over this superb hillside to find the Adonis Blue (which I did) and thus satiate my appetite for butterfly photography, and in the afternoon we would go to nearby Polesden Lacey where we satisfied Joan's appetite for historical architecture. Thankfully, the National Trust provided both these treats side-by-side.

Over recent years I have been able to combine visits to my elder son Mike with more Adonis Blue photography. Mike lives in Lewes in East Sussex, and just above his house on the northern edge of the Sussex Downs is a stretch of chalky grassland running alongside the town's golf course. This is a good butterfly site where I have taken many pictures of Adonis and Chalk-hill Blues. Surprisingly, my photographs, taken on 23 August 1997, show that this is not a closely-grazed greensward, but a rough jumble of bramble bushes, clumps of knapweed and plantains besides the requisite horseshoe vetch. Yet my son Mike has walked there regularly and has often seen Adonis Blues. Perhaps the *bellargus* breeding colonies lie at the very edges of this unkempt area, either where the golf course fairway is mown, or at the roadside which has a steep bank grazed by rabbits.

COMMON BLUE

The Common Blue *(Polyommatus icarus)* is a survivor – unlike its classical namesake Icarus, who fell into the Aegean Sea when his wings melted! This member of the *Lycaenidae* family is by far Europe's most widespread blue butterfly, occupying the whole of Continental Europe, Fennoscandia, temperate North Africa, the Middle East, the Mediterranean islands and the British Isles. In the colder climates it is single brooded, in southern Britain and central Europe it is double brooded, and in southern Europe it is triple brooded.

I have a collection of more than a hundred slides depicting the Common Blue. Rather in the manner of earlier collectors of dead specimens, my slides illustrate a number of colour variations in the female besides showing examples of very worn and tattered, yet still flying, Common Blues. I have also photographed these butterflies mating: on clover, on bramble, on birdsfoot trefoil, on dead knapweed flowerheads, on ribwort plantain and on grass. These pictures were taken, not for any voyeuristic reason but because they provide a useful comparison of the shape, size and colouring of the male and female seen side-by-side. For the photographer, *icarus* is a good subject and not camera shy.

My field records of the Common Blue, taken on a weekly basis during the butterfly season in West Harling Forest, span over a dozen years. They show that populations in 'my patch' vary widely from year to year. A typical annual count for the 1988 cycle shows: '28/5/88 – 2 males; 14/6/88 – 20 males + 3 females; 13/8/88 – 6 males; 31/8/88 – 22 (including mating pairs)'. In 1989 a first brood 'high' yielded: 'over 50' on 13 July. Three poor years followed, but numbers were back to fifty-plus in 1993. In 1995, good second broods were present until 21 September, and three good years followed, sometimes with a larger first brood, sometimes with the second brood numbers predominant. In 2000, both broods were numerous, exceeding sixty individuals. These figures are not particularly large but my patch includes only two rides in a large forest.

There are probably several reasons for these annual fluctuations, principally climatic variation year by year and forest management changes. Recently, I have noticed that several patches of the Common Blue's caterpillar food plant, birdsfoot trefoil, have disappeared, probably due to the overgrowth of surrounding grass, which has grown rapidly in the wetter weather of recent years. Also, the rabbit population, never large, seems to have vanished. To these factors may be added the drastic reduction in the regular mowing of the rides, perhaps a result of financial constraints, and the inadvertent stacking of logs on a former Common Blue breeding site. One must not forget however, that the plantations are a cash crop, and the main reason for much of the forest being there. In any case, Common Blues prosper in other parts of the forest, and some of the recently cleared areas will no doubt become colonised in coming years.

Lifesize

Male

Female

Male.
West Harling Forest, Norfolk
3rd June

Female.
West Harling Forest
3rd June

Female.
Brettenham Heath, Norfolk
17th August

Mating pair
Wingate Quarry, Co. Durham
August

COMMON BLUE

Polyommatus icarus

Female, lifesize

Male
Noar Hill,
Hampshire
25 May

Male
(Note reduced forelegs)
Noar Hill, Hampshire
24 May

DUKE OF BURGUNDY

Hamearis lucina

Female
Noar Hill, Hampshire
25 May

Female (Note forelegs fully developed)
Noar Hill, Hampshire
25 May

DUKE OF BURGUNDY

My diary page for 25 May 1993 gives a full account of a visit I made with my wife to Selborne in Hampshire, and our subsequent encounter with Duke of Burgundy *(Hamearis lucina)* butterflies. We had decided to have another of our dual interest days, this time a morning visit to Petworth House and the afternoon reserved for butterfly hunting on Noar Hill, south of Selborne. The diary starts with an entry concerning the paintings at Petworth. I wrote: 'Large portraits by Van Dyck, Lely and others are fine in small doses, but mounted two deep on every wall is a bit much, especially when surrounded by *trompe-l'oeil* vistas peopled by heroes, cherubs and cloud-borne virgins!' This was a bit cruel; I am sure that Joan took a more generous view.

Returning to butterflies, when we arrived at Noar Hill we were kindly guided to the Duke of Burgundy sites by two fellow butterfly watchers. This splendid, undulating area of meadow and scrub (formerly ancient chalkpits) was a mass of early purple orchids and cowslips. The cowslip is the principal food plant of the Duke of Burgundy caterpillar. When a suitable plant is found, the female perches on the edge of a leaf and, by curving her abdomen, lays an egg on the underside. We found many Dukes and had no trouble in identifying males from females by their behaviour. The males were aggressively defending their territories, and looked rather ragged from their persistence, while the females were sitting about looking pretty. Later, I discovered that the males have only four operative legs; the females have the usual six. (This is illustrated in the paintings at top right and bottom left).

The Duke of Burgundy Fritillary is something of an oddball in that it is the only European genus of the *Lycaenid* sub-family *Riodininae*, and is not really a fritillary at all, although in colour and patterning it looks like one. It is much smaller than the fritillaries, being about the size of the Small Copper. The main colonies of *lucina* are in the Cotswolds and Salisbury Plain, with a few scattered populations in North Yorkshire and north of Morecambe Bay in Cumbria. There may be unreported places where small numbers of *lucina* occupy very small sites. On 27 May 1987, I am certain that I saw a Duke of Burgundy sitting on a cowslip flower at the edge of a lightly-wooded farm track about a quarter of a mile from my home in East Harling, but several return visits proved fruitless. The butterfly is single brooded in Britain and is on the wing from early May until the last week of June. The eggs hatch in about a couple of weeks and the caterpillar feeds for a further six, after which the chrysalis remains hidden on the ground for ten months until the end of April the following year.

4

Nymphalidae:

Emperors & Admirals

White Admiral

Purple Emperor

Lesser Purple Emperor

Red Admiral

WHITE ADMIRAL

I count myself fortunate in living less than 3 kilometres from a forest where White Admirals *(Ladoga camilla)* are to be found each year. My records for the years 1988 to 2001 show that from the end of June until the third week of August, there is a good chance that I will have at least one sighting of a White Admiral, usually more than one. On twenty occasions I have been able to get close photographs of this butterfly in West Harling Forest, together with a further ten good shots in other woods nearby.

The White Admiral – now usually named *Limenitis camilla* – is often a rather elusive butterfly. When they are gliding in and out of the light and shade of a woodland canopy or flitting around bramble bushes, it is difficult to be certain of the number of individuals one is watching. For example, my logbook entry for 17 July 1991 remarks: '09.45 – 10.15hrs – 9 sightings; believe at least 4 different White Admirals'.

Some of my best observations of the behaviour of *camilla* have been made at what I call Reg Ransford's ride, a short woodland path on the western edge of the forest, along which my friend Reg regularly noted the presence of White Admirals when walking his dog. Almost every year, since he told me of this site, I have been there around the beginning of July, scanning the treetops and bramble bushes for a first sight of this graceful butterfly. They are quite splendid with their striking white wing bars and the wonderful orange and white undersurfaces, in stark contrast to the greenery of the woodland. The male butterflies are either prospecting the high canopy or patrolling the length of the ride with their strong, undulating flight, often returning to a favoured lookout branch which they will defend with vigour if challenged. Females seem to be rather more sedentary, often slowly exploring honeysuckle strands, or fluttering among the bramble flowers. Both male and female feed on aphid honeydew on the leaves of the high canopy, or nectar on bramble. Egg-laying takes place on the leaves of the larval food plant honeysuckle. After hatching, the caterpillar spends eleven months either eating or spending the cold months in its hibernaculum, a shelter which it has constucted from a honeysuckle leaf and silk supplied from its silk gland.

White Admirals occur in other parts of the forest. When seeking other sites I always bear in mind the main requirements for *camilla* to prosper: tall mature trees (usually oaks); sunshine and shade; honeysuckle; and bramble bushes. Although the White Admiral flourishes year after year in some parts of the forest, there is always the chance that encroaching conifer plantations will shut out the light. Indeed, this has happened during the past two years at Reg Ransford's ride where the bramble has been entirely shaded out, although the wonderful cascading honeysuckle still remains.

Male, lifesize

Male
West Harling Forest, Norfolk
17 July

Female
Knettishall Heath,
Suffolk
3 August

Male
West Harling Forest,
Norfolk
17 July

Newly-emerged male
Bernwood Forest, Oxford
19 July

WHITE ADMIRAL

Ladoga camilla

Male
Brodenbach, Germany
7th July

Male. lifesize

Male
Brodenbach, Germany
30th June

Male
Brodenbach, Germany
30th June

PURPLE EMPEROR

Apatura iris

Female, lifesize

PURPLE EMPEROR

My sole experience of the Purple Emperor *(Apatura iris)* in Britain lasted all of thirty seconds when a single male made a rapid circuit of a clearing in Bernwood Forest where I was standing, and then flew off in the hope of seeing something better. I knew at once from its flight and pattern that it was an Emperor, having watched this aristocratic butterfly many times in Germany. There, it is honoured by the name *Grosser Schillerfalter* after the revered German poet and dramatist, Schiller.

In July 1982 my wife and I spent the first of a number of holidays at Brodenbach on the River Mosel, about 20 kilometres upstream from Koblenz. Here, in two well-wooded valleys in the hills behind Brodenbach, we have often seen Emperors flitting among the oaks and sallows and, on several occasions, I have been able to photograph them at very close quarters. It is well known that these butterflies get most of their sustenance from aphid honeydew which they sip from the leaves of the woodland canopy, but the male Emperors may be seen imbibing nutrients from a wide variety of other sources. I have watched them, with their bright yellow proboscides uncoiled, sipping from wayside puddles; poking into the sticky syrup oozing from a damaged tree; sucking the juices from rotten fruit and from animal droppings; and even poking about in the ash of a barbecue pit! It has been occasions such as these that have allowed me to get really close to these butterflies, and to photograph the wonderful purplish blue sheen which is refracted from the wings of the males.

The stony footpaths in this limestone region, when washed by rain or small hillside streams, produce a mineral-rich cocktail on the surface of the ground, which probably provides essential nutrients for male butterflies. I have seen Purple Emperors, Lesser Purple Emperors, White Admirals, Commas and Silver-washed Fritillaries mud-puddling on the damp pathways. Alas, some of these paths have now been macadamised to provide more comfortable access for motorists to visit wayside inns. On later visits to these sites, we have noticed a remarkable drop in butterfly numbers where these paths have been resurfaced.

To illustrate further the extraordinary diet of male Purple Emperors, I record this interesting event. At a distance of about 3 kilometres from Brodenbach, along the valley called the Ehrenburgertal, lies a small hamlet with the imposing name of Brandengrabenmuhle. This is in the heart of Purple Emperor country and, when Joan and I made our way there on a hot July day we were glad to find a modest *Rasthaus* serving beer and snacks for passing walkers. Sitting there in the sunshine, we were joined at our table by a superb male Emperor. It sipped happily at a ring of beer from the glass of a previous drinker. It was no more than 10 centimetres from my hand and it stayed there long enough for me to finish my glass of Konigsbacher ale. Nearby stood a rusty old tractor beneath which was a puddle of engine oil and, lo and behold, there sat another Emperor, sipping oil!

LESSER PURPLE EMPEROR

The Lesser Purple Emperor *(Apatura ilia)* is found in the same type of habitat as its congener, the Purple Emperor. Both species inhabit mature, deciduous woodland with open clearings or rides, and in some cases they may share the same species of tree on which to lay their eggs. Usually this is sallow, although the Lesser Purple Emperor may prefer poplar when this grows locally. *Apatura ilia* does not occur in Britain, nor is it found in the northernmost parts of Europe or southern Italy. In the wooded hills near Brodenbach on the River Mosel, I have seen it flying at the same time as the Purple Emperor.

Distinguishing *ilia* from *iris* (the Purple Emperor) is not difficult. The Lesser Purple Emperor has more orange colouration than *iris*, and has a prominent orange circle on the upper and lower surfaces of the forewings. The male *ilia* sports the same purplish blue sheen as is seen on the wings of the male *iris*, but the female has no such iridescence. Most *ilia* populations contain some variants, usually *form clytie* where most of the white markings on the upper wing surface are replaced by orange. This is shown in the top right and middle left paintings opposite.

When Joan and I were watching these species in the woods near Brodenbach in 1981, we noticed that the Lesser Purple Emperors were usually seen at a lower layer of the trees than were the Purple Emperors, and I was able to photograph them half-hidden among the lower foliage. This may have been mere chance, and not have any behavioural significance. Certainly, we found *ilia* at ground level indulging in 'mud-puddling' or feeding on dung.

The presence of dog dirt has proved to be a useful aid to my obtaining close-up photographs of Emperors generally. By poking with a stick to 'rejuvenate' dried dog dirt, and then waiting patiently, the faecal stench soon attracts the butterflies down from the trees. Their preoccupation with feeding from the droppings allows one to approach quite closely. I have read accounts of the various kinds of bait put down by early butterfly collectors to attract the male Emperors (ripe or rotting fruit, dead mice and rabbits have been mentioned) and thought that I might try and make up an attractive potion. So I scrounged a few bits of salami and individual cartons of honey from the hotel breakfast table, and together with a can of Konigsbacher beer, made a rather watery paste which I smeared on a tree trunk. I waited for about ten minutes, noting that many flies were becoming interested in my concoction, when down swooped, not an Emperor, but a rather larger Poplar Admiral *(Limenitis populi)* which took one sniff and fluttered away! No chance of taking a photograph, but at least I had seen a new species of butterfly.

Female, lifesize

LESSER PURPLE EMPEROR

Apatura ilia

Female (f. clyte)
Brodenbach, Germany
13th July

Male (f. clyte)
Spanish Pyrenees
10th June

Male (on dung)
Brodenbach,
6th. July

Female
Brodenbach,
6th. July

Male, lifesize

West Harling Forest,
23rd August

East Harling,
19th September

West Harling Forest,
29th August

RED ADMIRAL

Vanessa atalanta

RED ADMIRAL

Ican think of no butterfly with a more military appearance than the Red Admiral *(Vanessa atalanta)*. Whenever I inspect one closely, perched on my buddleia in the late summer sunshine, I cannot help but marvel at its smartness from the tips of its antennae to the 'blue buttons' on its coat-tails! Seen from above, its colour scheme has no subtle shades, only bold statements of black, crimson, white and tiny spots of blue. The whole upperside appearance suggests a uniform – perhaps an artilleryman at Waterloo or a present-day Royal Marine in dress uniform. On its undersurfaces however, things are different; although the forewings echo the topside patterns, the hindwings are its camouflage dress. With its wings closed and only the hindwing showing, it is virtually impossible to spot when close against a tree trunk or among autumn foliage.

My slide collection contains some seventy pictures of the Red Admiral, mostly taken in Norfolk, but including others taken in distant Northumberland and Devon. Almost all the photographs were taken in August and ninety per cent were taken in gardens. Indeed, my field logbook shows few sightings of the Red Admiral in the forest.

It is now recognised that the Red Admirals we see (often in abundance) in August are almost all immigrants from southern Europe, or the progeny of Admirals which came into Britain in May or June or later, as the immigrants start laying their eggs on nettle soon after their arrival. The few butterflies that attempt to overwinter in trees or garden sheds rarely survive.

I have often studied the behaviour of the Red Admiral in the summer evenings when they bask in the fading sunshine before departing to their nocturnal hiding places. Some bask on the gravel or on the concrete paths with their wings outstretched to receive radiant heat from the remaining sunshine, but at the same time with the trailing edges of their hindwings touching the ground to retain reflected heat from the warm stones. This is necessary if the butterfly is to keep the flight muscles attached to its thorax warm, so that it remains capable of instant flight. In the same way, Red Admirals can be observed standing head down, with wings tightly closed, on a warm fence post in the evening sunshine. Here, they are conserving body heat in the envelope formed between body and closed wings, the hairs on the thorax contributing towards this essential retention of heat.

To watch Red Admirals nectaring on buddleia is interesting. The long proboscis, with its convenient 'knee joint', is ideally suited to probing the deep corolla of the buddleia floret. I have often wondered at the extraordinary accuracy with which this butterfly aims the tip of its proboscis plumb in the centre of the corolla tube. In my garden, the Red Admiral also feeds on globe thistle and Michaelmas daisy. In the forest it is usually found on knapweed.

5

Nymphalidae:

VANESSIDS

SMALL TORTOISESHELL

PEACOCK

PAINTED LADY

COMMA

SMALL TORTOISESHELL

The Small Tortoiseshell *(Aglais urticae)* is a very successful and widespread butterfly. Its range extends across Continental Europe and Asia as far as the Pacific coast, and it is a familiar sight throughout the British Isles. It is one of four British butterflies that routinely hibernate as an adult during the colder months of the year, the others being Brimstone, Peacock and Comma. I have often found hibernating Tortoiseshells in my garage or garden shed, and sometimes even within the house, where I once photographed one in deep hibernation with its antennae tucked into its folded wings.

The Small Tortoiseshell is often the first butterfly I see in the garden in late February or early March, when I find it taking nectar from heather flowers or basking in the late winter sunshine. I welcome it as the herald of a new butterfly year! During the following weeks the butterfly will take advantage of fine weather to feed and find a mate. I have watched, and photographed, courting behaviour on two occasions: once in early April 1982 on a nettle bed, and on 13 March 1993 on the leaves of red hot poker plants. In both cases the male was standing immediately behind the female, and shaking his open wings rapidly. Presumably, he was wafting pheromones onto the female as an aphrodisiac. This wing shivering lasted for several minutes before the pair descended into the depths of the plant. Mating takes place secretly, deep in the nettle patch. The painting in the centre of the page opposite illustrates pre-mating behaviour. The female is slightly larger than the male, although the difference in size is somewhat exaggerated in this picture owing to the foreshortened angle of the male butterfly.

The female lays her eggs on common nettle after carefully selecting a suitable young, tender plant in a sunny location. Eggs, usually in large numbers, are laid on the underside of a leaf. They hatch in about a fortnight and the mass of tiny caterpillars immediately spin a silken web over the leaf tips which, in the nettle, are suitably notched to provide anchoring points for the silk. The caterpillars remain gregarious until they reach their final size, when they become independent. Pupation takes place some distance from their natal nettle bed. Chrysalids are usually very handsome, often becoming a shining gold colour. The emerging butterflies will constitute the summer brood; the earlier ones will reproduce quickly, those emerging later in the summer will spend the winter in a state of suspended development and will have to wait until the following spring to breed.

Populations of the Small Tortoiseshell fluctuate from year to year and are very dependent on weather conditions, particularly in spring. In my collection of slides of the Small Tortoiseshell, I have many pictures of large numbers of the butterflies nectaring on ice plants. These pictures were taken over several years but, alas, over the past two summers the tortoiseshells have not appeared, though the ice plants have flowered as normal. I believe that the very wet winter weather we have suffered during 2000 and 2001 may have been responsible for a dramatic fall in tortoiseshell numbers. Low temperatures during hibernation do not bother them, but prolonged exposure to damp conditions often proves fatal. However, the wet weather during the 2000/2001 winters may not have been the only cause of their decline, disease or parasites may have been responsible.

SMALL TORTOISESHELL

Aglais urticae

Female, lifesize

'Courting' pair
Ponteland, Northumberland
15 April

East Harling, Norfolk
10 September

East Harling, Norfolk
4 September

Male, lifesize

West Harling Forest, Norfolk
20th August

East Harling, Norfolk
22nd August

West Harling Forest, Norfolk
9th September

PEACOCK

Inachis io

PEACOCK

I described the colour scheme of the Red Admiral as being like a military uniform; using a similar analogy, the Peacock's *(Inachis io)* magnificent colours and patterns must surely be described as theatrical – a pantomime display, and a joy to paint!

The large eye shapes, staring owl-like from the upper surfaces of all four wings, must startle a potential predator when the wings are suddenly opened. What an effective means of defence, especially when accompanied by the butterfly's ability to make a loud, hissing noise by rubbing its wings together! In contrast, the dark wing undersides, looking like charred wood, provide a perfect camouflage when the butterfly is hiding against a tree trunk.

The Peacock is essentially a woodland butterfly, although we recognise it as a garden companion when we see it on our late summer flowers. It spends the winter months of the year hibernating among trees – indeed, *within* trees if suitable cracks and crevices can be found. Sometimes these butterflies will use a hollow tree as a communal night-time roosting place, feeding during the late summer days until they begin their winter sleep.

Peacock butterflies are seen early in the spring. My earliest sighting was on 6 February 1987 when I saw one flying across a street in the centre of Thetford, probably having had its hibernation disturbed. Normally, they are first seen in April along the forest rides, feeding on ground ivy, dandelion or garlic mustard, or merely basking on a warm stone or piece of wood. At this time, males can be seen jousting with other males in an attempt to secure their territory, or they may be chasing females.

Egg-laying begins in May. I have been able to photograph their green eggs piled in a tidy heap on the underside of a stinging nettle leaf during my visits to local fen woodland, and a week or so later watch the black, wriggling mass of young caterpillars breaking free of their silken crèche, dispersing, then spinning fresh webs before eventually departing to feed independently. In June, I found and photographed a fully-grown caterpillar hanging beneath a nettle leaf, preparing to pupate.

From mid-July the new brood of Peacocks begin to appear, often in large numbers. My records for 1999 give a typical emergence pattern for my patch in West Harling Forest. On 20 July I counted just two; on 23 July there were ten; on 28 July I recorded more than thirty; on 29 July, more than fifty; on 4 August I wrote 'many, perhaps 100'; on 23 August there were more than fifteen; and finally, my last record on 27 August noted 'about 10'. I did not see any Peacocks after that date. A similar pattern of sightings was recorded in 2000.

PAINTED LADY

The Painted Lady *(Cynthia cardui)* is both extraordinarily prolific and a great traveller. In some years millions of these butterflies leave their main breeding grounds in North Africa and Arabia and surge northwards in great swarms, often travelling hundreds of kilometres to find feeding and breeding places across Europe and Fennoscandia. Although this butterfly is a strong flyer, Continental weather systems can affect its eventual destination. For example, in the notable migration of the Painted Lady to Britain in 1980, the clockwise winds around a large high pressure system over central Europe brought a large influx into the Western Isles and Wales in early June. A further large invasion, which arrived in late July, brought the butterflies across the North Sea on the winds around an anticyclone centred over Scandinavia. From their landfall on the east coast they quickly spread inland, eventually invading every county of Britain. It was in August 1980 that I photographed my first Painted Lady butterflies at Middleton-in-Teesdale where they were nectaring on spear thistle.

Records show that, over the past sixty years, the Painted Lady has been a regular visitor, although its numbers fluctuate widely. My records show that in my part of East Anglia 1996 was a good *cardui* year. During a dry period in June I walked along Fen Lane, near where I live in the village of East Harling, looking for butterflies. At the end of the lane where it enters woodland, I found that the large pond was completely dried out, although the ground was still soft underfoot. Covering the entire basin-shaped depression where the pond had been was a dense carpet of hedge mustard in full flower. The flowerheads were alive with Painted Lady butterflies. I decided to try and count them but when I reached ninety-seven, and had by no means scanned the whole area, I found myself unable to breathe properly, so great was the amount of pollen in the air. With streaming eyes I retraced my steps! This was certainly a good time to see *Cynthia cardui*. Three days earlier I had counted over seventy of these attractive butterflies during a walk around my patch in the forest.

The Painted Lady breeds rapidly; the stages of development between egg-laying and pupation can take less than a month during warm weather. The female lays her eggs on a variety of plants, such as mallows, nettles and, most usually, thistles. Viper's bugloss has also been recorded as a larval food plant and, because I find this plant growing profusely on my patch in the forest and it is greatly favoured by feeding *cardui* butterflies, I must search its leaves for eggs. These are laid singly on the upper sides of the leaves of the host plant, but the young caterpillars move beneath the leaf to feed in the safety of a silken web which they have woven.

Female, lifesize

East Harling, Norfolk
23rd August

Budle Bay, Northumberland
10th September

PAINTED LADY

Cynthia cardui

Lifesize

West Harling Forest, Norfolk
5th August

East Harling, Norfolk
8th September

Bridgham Heath, Norfolk
29th April

COMMA

Polygonia c-album

COMMA

I admit to having a particular affection for the Comma butterfly *(Polygonia c-album)*. Its bizarre, ragged outline and its mottled cryptic underside, complete with the bright white comma-shaped trademark, render it unique among our British butterflies.

The sunshine of early spring tempts me to visit a nearby copse with a wide clearing where, amongst the leaf litter spread by winter winds, I can usually find a Comma newly awakened from its long hibernation. As the butterfly sits there, it is interesting to watch its efforts to maintain its body heat by half-closing its wings to shield its thorax from the cool wind. Now and again it will momentarily spread its wings to absorb the sun's rays. During this period of heat regulation it is loth to fly away, and one can approach quite closely. I have developed a simple method whereby I can inspect the butterfly in detail. If I gently put a forefinger alongside the Comma whilst its wings are closed, in most cases the butterfly will climb onto the finger, sensing the extra warmth, and remain there whilst I raise my hand for a closer look!

When fully active, the Comma flies vigorously along the forest rides. Its purposeful pursuit of a male rival, or its hectic chasing of a female, makes it easy to spot even from a distance.

I have a collection of over fifty slides illustrating the Comma, ranging from middle-distance shots showing it among bramble flowers or drinking sap from a tree wound, to ultra close-up pictures showing its proboscis plunging deep into a buddleia floret. Looking through these pictures has enabled me readily to identify the darker (normal) form of *c-album* from the paler golden form *hutchinsoni* which emerge from early June pupation. It is interesting to note that the dark camouflage pattern on the underwing of the normal form (an obvious asset during hibernation) is not present on the lighter, buff-coloured underwings of *hutchinsoni*, which does not hibernate.

My logbook shows that year-by-year the Comma is seen in West Harling Forest from mid-April to late September with a gap during June when the adult Commas are absent. Two interesting entries are: 'Saturday 18 April 1987, Ride 80 (TL978837) 12 Comma *(P. c-album)* – some "jousting" pairs and others defending their territories against five Peacocks *(I.io).*' and 'Sunday 24 September 1989, Ride 52 Higher Bridgham Plantation (TL 942858) about 40 Comma *(P. c-album)* and 12 Red Admiral *(V. atalanta)* – noted resting on trunks of Scots pine and basking in the evening sunshine. Some feeding on tree wounds.'

6
Nymphalidae:

FRITILLARIES

SILVER-WASHED FRITILLARY

CARDINAL

DARK GREEN FRITILLARY

HIGH BROWN FRITILLARY

QUEEN OF SPAIN FRITILLARY

PEARL-BORDERED FRITILLARY

SMALL PEARL-BORDERED FRITILLARY

GLANVILLE FRITILLARY

HEATH FRITILLARY

MARSH FRITILLARY

SILVER-WASHED FRITILLARY

My experience of the Silver-washed Fritillary *(Argynnis paphia)* was first gained in Germany during two holidays at Brodenbach in the Mosel region in the early 1980s. In the butterfly-rich woodlands lying between the Moselle and the Rhine, my wife and I had the pleasure of many sightings of this graceful butterfly gliding and wheeling in dappled sunlight along forest rides. Sometimes, where the paths were damp with overnight rain or morning dew, we were able to watch male Fritillaries sipping the moisture in company with other woodland species. Our German holidays yielded good photographs. Later, in August 1991, we were able to get more pictures of *paphia* in England when we found them in Tugley Wood in Hampshire, and at Puddledown Forest in Dorset. In 1994 we were able to renew our aquaintance with this Fritillary in the woods above Brodenbach, where I received several pats on the back from passing walkers when I told them, in my schoolboy German, that I loved studying the wonderful German butterflies!

The male Silver-washed Fritillary is readily distinguished from the female when viewed from above: males have black streaks alongside their main wing veins, resulting from a heavy deposit of black androconial scales from which pheromones are emitted during courtship display. Females are slightly larger and have more extensive black spots against a duller orange ground colour. The undersides of both sexes display silver streaks against moss green markings. These are the silver washes that give the butterfly its name.

The larval food plant of the Silver-washed Fritillary is violet, usually the common dog violet which carpets the ground wherever there is sufficient light for it to flourish. The female butterflies do not lay their eggs on the leaves of the violet, as one might expect, but in crevices or on patches of moss on the trunks of nearby trees, a metre or more above ground level. The caterpillars, on hatching, immediately begin their hibernation on the tree trunk, and not until the following spring do they descend to feed on the dog violets.

In Britain the Silver-washed Fritillaries appear in early July. They are confined to discrete colonies in mature woodland in counties south-west of a line drawn from North Wales to Kent. There are also scattered colonies in Ireland, and in isolated locations in the Midlands and Cumbria. In Devon and Cornwall they may be found on the high banks bordering minor roads, where they occupy a much more open habitat. In this situation, the eggs are laid on hedgerow twigs or patches of moss.

The Silver-washed Fritillary has suffered a decline in many parts of its range since the 1970s, though its disappearance has not been as dramatic as the decline of the other woodland Fritillaries, the Pearl-bordered, the Small Pearl-bordered and the High Brown.

Lifesize

Male

Female

Female. Tualey Wood, Hampshire
August

Male, drinking dew at
roadside.
Brodenbach, Germany
July

SILVER-WASHED FRITILLARY

Argynnis paphia

Male. Puddletown Forest, Dorset
14 August

Male, lifesize

Male
Mljet, Yugoslavia
28th June

Male
Mljet, Yugoslavia
27th June

Female
Mljet, Yugoslavia
26th June

Female, Mljet, Yugoslavia
26th June

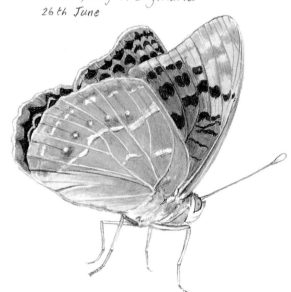

CARDINAL

Argynnis pandora

CARDINAL

We must return to the Adriatic island of Mljet for a description of this Fritillary – the Cardinal *(Argynnis pandora)*. As its generic name implies, it is a near relation of the Silver-washed Fritillary to which it has a superficial resemblance. Indeed, on the rare occasions when this butterfly has turned up in southern England (near Tintagel in Cornwall, and near Lulworth Cove in Dorset) it was thought to be either a Silver-washed Fritillary or a Dark Green Fritillary, only later was it correctly identified as *A. pandora*.

In my notes about the Swallowtail, I mentioned that Joan and I had seen Cardinals, in company with Swallowtails and Cleopatras, gorging themselves on thistles near our hotel on the island. Whilst I was happily photographing the Swallowtails, I decided to save some film for the Cardinals and took eleven close-up shots for my collection. So preoccupied were the butterflies with sipping the juices of the thistles, that they completely ignored the near presence of a mere photographer. The thistles in question are worth a mention. They are the spectacular milk thistle which flourish profusely in the Mediterranean region, and are particularly favoured by butterflies. My painting (lower right) shows a female Cardinal ensconced on a milk thistle flowerhead.

If we compare the Cardinal with the Silver-washed Fritillary we find several points of difference: the Cardinal is slightly larger than *A. paphia*; the male has only two black-bordered veins (sex brands) to the three on the upper surfaces of the male *paphia*; the ground colour of the Cardinal's upper surfaces is greenish-orange, especially on the hind wings; and on the green undersides, the silver-washed marks are reduced to mere streaks of silver on the Cardinal. The main recognition feature, however, is the large patch of rose-red in the discal area of the underside of the forewings, which is suggestive of the red robes of a cardinal, hence the vernacular name of the butterfly.

The geographical distribution of the Cardinal is more southern than that of the Silver-washed Fritillary. It is not present in northern Europe, but is found in the South of France, Spain and North Africa; the Mediterranean islands and southern Italy; southern Austria and the Balkans; Greece and the Greek islands.

In common with all the *Nymphalidae* butterflies, the Fritillaries are sometimes called 'brush-footed' butterflies because of the fine hairs on their vestigial legs. These redundant legs are all that remain of what served as their forelegs in the distant past, when the butterfly was six-legged. They are now reduced to mere swellings tucked up against the thorax and extending from the leg socket (just in front of what are now the butterfly's forelegs) diagonally upwards to a point behind the eye. The vestigial legs may be seen in two paintings opposite at top right and bottom left.

DARK GREEN FRITILLARY

This butterfly is an old friend. My earliest photographs of the Dark Green Fritillary *(Argynnis aglaja)* were taken in June 1979 on Holy Island (Lindisfarne) off the Northumberland coast. At that time I was a keen bird-watcher, more interested in the bar-tailed godwit than butterflies. However, during my summer birding visits to that part of the coast, I came to notice the presence of an attractive orange-coloured butterfly with black spots on its wings flying among the marram grass and sand dunes. Thus my future interest in butterflies was kindled.

There were many Dark Green Fritillaries on the northern shores of Holy Island, and I remember thinking how much more interesting it was to watch these lovely creatures basking on the silver sand of the dunes than peering seawards through binoculars searching for some distant surf scoters or long-tailed ducks! My logbook entry for 23 July 1983 notes: 'Holy Island. Dark Green Fritillaries *(Argynnis aglaja)* abundant – 50+ between NU129434 and NU135435 – most specimens were faded and frayed'. They were obviously past their best at this date. In addition, I also recorded seeing several hundred Grayling and Meadow Brown butterflies in the same area.

At that time, I assumed that *A. aglaja* was a coastal butterfly until I learned of its wide distribution throughout Britain, including a separate subspecies in Scotland. Following a considerable decline in downland populations, the butterfly's strongest bastions nowadays are on the coast where unimproved grassland is most often found. In most downland populations, the eggs are laid on hairy violet; in the few woodland colonies the dog violet is used; and on Holy Island and other damp locations, the larval food plant is marsh violet. The caterpillars hibernate through the cold months, not feeding until the spring when they eat their food plants. They become fully grown and ready for pupation in May. Then the caterpillar makes a canopy of leaves drawn together by threads of silk from which it hangs as a chrysalis. The butterflies emerge in mid-June.

The photographs I took on Holy Island and places nearby show the Dark Green Fritillaries nectaring on creeping thistle, ragwort, viper's bugloss and red clover, but I have also seen them feeding at ground level on carline thistle. My paintings were based on these photographs. The lovely dark green shading and the silver 'pearls' can be seen on the two lower paintings.

♂ Lifesize

♀ Holy Island, Northumberland
August

DARK GREEN FRITILLARY

Argynnis aglaja

Budle Bay,
Northumberland
Late June

♂
Holy Island,
Northumberland
1st August

Male, Arnside Knott, Lancashire
July

Male, lifesize

Male
Arnside Knott, Lancashire
July

Female
Arnside Knott, Lancashire
July

Female
Arnside Knott
July

HIGH BROWN FRITILLARY

Argynnis adippe

HIGH BROWN FRITILLARY

In July 1982 Joan and I visited Arnside Knott, a National Trust reserve at the north-east corner of Morecambe Bay. We were both looking forward to revisiting this corner of Cumbria, especially as we hoped to find one of Britain's most endangered butterflies – the High Brown Fritillary *(Argynnis adippe)*. Arnside Knott is an area of open woodland, with bracken and scrubby bushes including large bramble bushes. This is a limestone region with quite large slabs protruding among the vegetation. We parked the car and walked up to the higher parts of the reserve. Joan found a pleasant, sunny spot with a seat, whilst I wandered about looking for *adippe*. I soon spotted a couple flying rapidly over the high bracken and shortly afterwards was able to photograph one feeding on knapweed, and another basking on bramble leaves.

Fine, I had got two good close-up shots of what I assumed to be High Brown Fritillaries, but they may have been Dark Green Fritillaries, which I had been told to expect there as well as *adippe*. Both have similar upper wing patterns. What I needed was a picture of the underside of the wings showing the row of reddish-brown spots characteristic of the High Brown. I guessed that the only way that I could be certain of getting such a shot was to kneel down beside a bramble bush and wait until a Fritillary approached the flowers above my head. It was then that I experienced one of the hardships of photographing butterflies.

A few moments after I had taken up my vantage point, a young man in running gear flopped down on the other side of the bramble bush, quite oblivious of my presence. I could hear him panting after his run. Suddenly, he stood up, pulled down his shorts and underpants and started examining himself! I dared not move. Only a few feet of bramble bush separated us, and I had no wish to surprise him. I began to get cramp in my legs, and the minutes dragged. After about five minutes he covered his nether regions and trotted off. Seconds later, a High Brown Fritillary landed just above my head and I was able to get the picture I wanted. I could have been spared all this anguish because, several minutes later, Joan spotted another *adippe* standing on the path with its wings closed and showing its underwing markings to perfection, and I was able to photograph it. My paintings are based on these shots.

I am conscious that I have used this page to write more about human behaviour than butterfly behaviour, but I feel it is important to mention some of the perils of watching butterflies. One is seen crouching among bracken; staring at the treetops; rushing in pursuit of a tiny insect; probing about in bushes looking for caterpillars. Normal people walking in the woods don't behave in this way! I have heard worried mothers say to their children: 'Come away from that awful man. You don't know what he's up to!'

QUEEN OF SPAIN FRITILLARY

I had to wait several years between my first seeing a Queen of Spain Fritillary *(Issoria lathonia)* and assembling a sufficient number of photographs from which to make representative paintings of this butterfly. My logbook shows that I saw Queen of Spain Fritillaries on 13 July 1994 in the woods above Brodenbach, in the Mosel district of Germany. I can recall these sightings clearly. I was standing beside a 1.5 metre-high bramble bush on which were feeding many Silver-washed Fritillaries, White Admirals and one or two Map butterflies, when I noticed an oddball among the Fritillaries – a 'squarish' sort of Fritillary which, as it moved around the bramble flowers, revealed a flash of large silver 'pearls' on its underside. With the camera at the ready, I moved in for a quick shot – the picture which I later used to make the painting shown opposite at lower left.

Some ten minutes later, further along the forest path, I found another Queen of Spain nicely posed on a bramble leaf. This second shot formed the basis of the painting at bottom right.

Not until 18 June 2001, when I went to the Spanish Pyrenees, did I get a chance to augment those earlier pictures. My guide, Paul Cardy, knew several places where the *lathonia* butterflies could be found. At one site, two or three were seen feeding on a species of elder which was heavy with white, globular flowers. This plant was certainly a favourite with butterflies which gathered around it for hours on end. It was ideal for photography too, being just the right height for eye-level viewing. The picture I painted (top right) is based on a photograph I took at the time. During my week in the Spanish Pyrenees we encountered the Queen of Spain Fritillary on four days, seeing it several times nectaring in flower-filled meadows.

This butterfly is a vagrant visitor to England, occuring only rarely in September, and usually confined to the most southern counties. Inexplicably, it has not established itself anywhere in Britain, whereas it is resident in southern Sweden, Finland, the Netherlands and throughout Europe.

I have referred to this butterfly's appearance as squarish, and this is the general impression when it is seen from above. There are two reasons for this: the edges of the forewings are slightly concave (not convex as in most butterflies) and the trailing edges of the hindwings, when held together alongside the body, form a straight line, rather than being rounded as is usual in other species. This can be seen in the picture at lower right.

Male, lifesize

QUEEN OF SPAIN FRITILLARY

Issoria lathonia

Female,
Spanish Pyrenees
18th June

Female,
Spanish Pyrenees   20th June

Male,
Brodenbach/Mosel
13th July

Female,
Brodenbach/Mosel
13th July

PEARL-BORDERED FRITILLARY

Boloria euphrosyne

Lifesize

Male

Female
Silverdale, Lancashire
late May. 1981

Male. Silverdale, Lancashire
late May, 1981

Male
Salzkammergut, Austria
late June, 1988

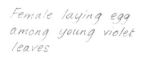

Female laying egg
among young violet
leaves

PEARL-BORDERED FRITILLARY

ooking at the distribution maps of the Fritillary butterflies published in *The Millennium Atlas of Butterflies in Britain and Ireland* one becomes quite depressed, as a person living in East Anglia, at the almost total absence of red dots denoting records of Fritillaries in our region. Indeed, apart from a few records of the Dark Green Fritillary on the Norfolk coast, almost the whole of eastern England is bereft of Fritillaries. This has not always been the case. If one studies the (sometimes rather vague) distribution maps in such a book as Edmund Sandars' *A Butterfly Book for the Pocket*, published in 1939, the maps show *all* the Fritillaries (except the Glanville and the Heath) as being resident in East Anglia! That this remarkable change of fortune has taken place in about sixty years is saddening.

My attempts to obtain photographic records of the Pearl-bordered Fritillary *(Boloria euphrosyne)* have required me to journey afar. When I lived in Northumberland, the nearest Fritillary country lay in Cumbria and was not too distant, merely a question of following Hadrian's Wall and turning left at the end of it! So it has been in northwest England, and a place abroad, where I have got my *euphrosyne* pictures.

In May 1981, in company with my friend Peter West, I visited a site adjacent to a caravan park near Silverdale on the Cumbria/Lancashire border. Here we found the Pearl-bordered Fritillary among limestone rocks in a hollow near light woodland. In a short time I was able to get three good pictures: one of a male basking on the rocks, a shot of a female perched on a bramble leaf, and a third picture which turned out to be a Small Pearl-bordered Fritillary *(Boloria selene)* (see the next entry).

Seven years later, in June 1988, whilst exploring a nature reserve in the Salzkammergut region of Austria, Joan spotted a Pearl-bordered Fritillary walking on a patch of sphagnum moss which provided me with a good side view of the butterfly, and a short time later I found a female ovipositing on violet leaves. This is illustrated in the lower right painting opposite.

This delightful, low-flying butterfly brings brightness and colour to a woodland clearing in the spring and early summer or, less obviously, it may be found basking in the sunshine on a carpet of dead bracken, the colour of which it nearly matches.

To distinguish between this butterfly and its similar congener, *selene*, a side view provides the best opportunity. In *euphrosyne*, at the centre of the underside of the hindwing, is a large pearl patch, with a smaller pearl in front of it. In the case of the Small Pearl-bordered Fritillary, there are many more pearly shapes on the underside of its hindwing. Both species sport the row of seven pearls along the wing edge.

SMALL PEARL-BORDERED FRITILLARY

The Small Pearl-bordered Fritillary *(Boloria selene)* can be confused in the field with its close relative, the Pearl-bordered Fritillary *(Boloria euphrosyne)*. Although *selene* emerges about a month later than *euphrosyne*, they can be seen on the wing together as their flight periods overlap. When seen as a mixed group, the orange ground colour of the newer *selene* will appear slightly darker than that of the *euphrosyne* which will have lost scales with time, and appear faded. In my notes about the Pearl-bordered Fritillary, I mentioned the most obvious features for differentiation between the two species: the number of bright pearl shapes on the underside of the hindwings. When viewing the butterflies from above, they can sometimes be separated by looking at the row of black markings immediately inside the outer edges of the wings. In *euphrosyne* they are usually black triangles; in *selene* they are black chevrons.

The two species have slightly different habitat requirements for egg-laying: the Pearl-bordered prefers warm, bare ground where young violets grow in dry, sunny situations; the Small Pearl-bordered often chooses much damper places where the violets are found among taller, lusher vegetation, although it also breeds on moorland and moist grassland. Both species use the common dog-violet or, in the north or in wet habitats, the marsh violet. The caterpillars feed on their food plants for several weeks, before hibernating in the vegetation until the following spring.

This butterfly has a northern inclination, with a much wider distribution in Scotland, northwest England and Wales than does *euphrosyne*. This northerly tendency is echoed in Europe where *selene* does not occur south of the Alps, nor in the Balkans and Greece where *euphrosyne* is common.

It will be seen from the pencilled notes on the paintings that I took my reference photographs in the Morecambe Bay area, with the exception of the one taken in Austria. The male shown top left is unusual in having diminished black markings, although they are not as reduced as occurs in the aberration *obsoleta*.

Female, lifesize

Male.
Silverdale, Lancashire
late May

Female
Salzkammergut,
Austria.
early July

SMALL PEARL-BORDERED FRITILLARY

Boloria selene

Male
Arnside Knott, Cumbria
June

Female
Arnside Knott, Cumbria
June

Male, lifesize

Female
Compton Chine I.O.W
27 May

Mottestone Down, I.O.W
26 May

Male
Compton Chine I.O.W
27 May

Male
Compton Chine I.O.W
27 May

GLANVILLE FRITILLARY

Melitaea cinxia

GLANVILLE FRITILLARY

In Britain, this Fritillary is restricted to a few places in the south of the Isle of Wight. It is named after Lady Eleanor Glanville who was the first person to capture British specimens, in Lincolnshire, in the late seventeenth century. Because of its present confined location in the extreme south of England, we may be inclined to think of it as an extremely rare butterfly. This is not the case. The Glanville Fritillary *(Melitaea cinxia)* has a very wide range right across Europe, stretching from southern Fennoscandia to Sicily, and from the Spanish Pyrenees to Greece and Turkey. I have photographed it at Lipica, in Slovenia, and in the Spanish Pyrenees, but I prize more dearly those pictures I took on the Isle of Wight, where it has been recorded since 1824.

My diary entries for 26 and 27 May 1992 describe how I got my first sighting of *cinxia*. Joan and I had decided to have a three-day break at Freshwater Bay in the hope that the promising weather forecast would give us the chance to find these Fritillaries. I wrote: 'As soon as we drove off the ferry at Yarmouth, in bright sunshine, I suggested that we should drive at once to Compton Chine, as we had read that this was a good place to find the Glanville Fritillary. I first stopped at a car park below Compton Down, where I found a young National Trust warden whom I questioned about the exact location of *cinxia*. Our spirits fell when he told us that it looked like being a very poor year for Glanvilles, as he hadn't seen any. However, he kindly offered to walk over to the Chine and let us know if he could spot any. He returned with the good news that he had seen one!'

Joan left me to undertake the rather perilous scramble along the undercliff, while she found a comfortable seat. Working my way cautiously along the crumbling ground I was able to find and photograph six *cinxia*. They were very wily, and not easy to approach, but they prefer this rough undercliff where their larval food plant ribwort plantain grows in abundance. The undercliff also supports nectar-rich plants, such as thrift and birdsfoot trefoil, on which the butterflies feed.

The next day, I took more pictures of the Glanville Fritillary on the undercliff at Compton Chine, on Compton Down and on Mottestone Down. They are quite easy to identify by the row of orange squares, each with a black dot in the centre, seen just above the orange crescent-shaped marks on the outer border of the hindwing. These are seen in the paintings of the plan views opposite, on the right.

In the field, the male butterflies are particularly restless and active when they are patrolling the shore looking for females with which they may mate. When they mate, they may be seen flying in tandem with the female dragging along the male while she looks for a suitable clump of young plantains on which to lay her eggs, after abandoning her partner!

HEATH FRITILLARY

At the end of June 1989, my wife and I celebrated my early retirement by organising a motoring holiday in Austria. We planned to combine butterfly hunting with visits to towns and cities where we could learn something about Austria's history. As a means of making the most of our time, before embarking from Dover, we spent a pleasant afternoon in East Blean Woods photographing the Heath Fritillary *(Mellicta athalia)*. A couple of days later, at a nature reserve, near Neukirchen in the Salzkammergut, we were again taking pictures of the Heath Fritillary.

In contrast to the situation in Kent, where these Fritillaries are confined to managed clearings in the woods and there is no doubt about their identity, in Europe Fritillaries of many different species are to be found, and sorting the Heath Fritillaries from those of similar size, pattern and colour is not easy. At one point I was taking shots of two Fritillaries indulging in courtship behaviour. They were facing each other, touching each other's wing edges with the clubs of their antennae. I thought that they were Heath Fritillaries, but on getting the slides back from processing, I found that one of the butterflies was not a Heath Fritillary but a False Heath Fritillary *(Melitaea diamina)*! This was an interesting picture in itself, but also an example of the identification problems which may arise in places where many different species of Fritillary occupy the same flowery meadow. During my recent butterfly holiday in the Spanish Pyrenees, we visited several such meadows and logged nineteen different species of Fritillary. I would have been able to identify less than half of them, but thanks to the knowledge of my guide and mentor, Paul Cardy, I was given the name of each one.

Alas, the situation in England, so far as the Heath Fritillary is concerned, is quite different. The excellent publication *The Millennium Atlas of Butterflies in Britain and Ireland* tells the story of the dramatic decline of this species and of the determined attempts to maintain and improve its scant representation on the British list. At present, the colonies in East Blean Woods are being assisted by providing clearings where the caterpillar's food plant, common cow-wheat, can continue to flourish; reintroduction of the Heath Fritillary at two coppiced woods in Essex has proved successful; and the conservation measures taken by the National Trust and others to preserve the species in the valleys of Exmoor and elsewhere in Devon offer some hope for the future. On the acid soils of the latter, the larval food plants are different. Here, ribwort plantain or germander speedwell provide the caterpillar food.

My paintings show three representative specimens from East Blean Woods, and an illustration of an Italian *athalia* which kindly posed for my camera on the slopes of Monte Baldo, above Lake Garda.

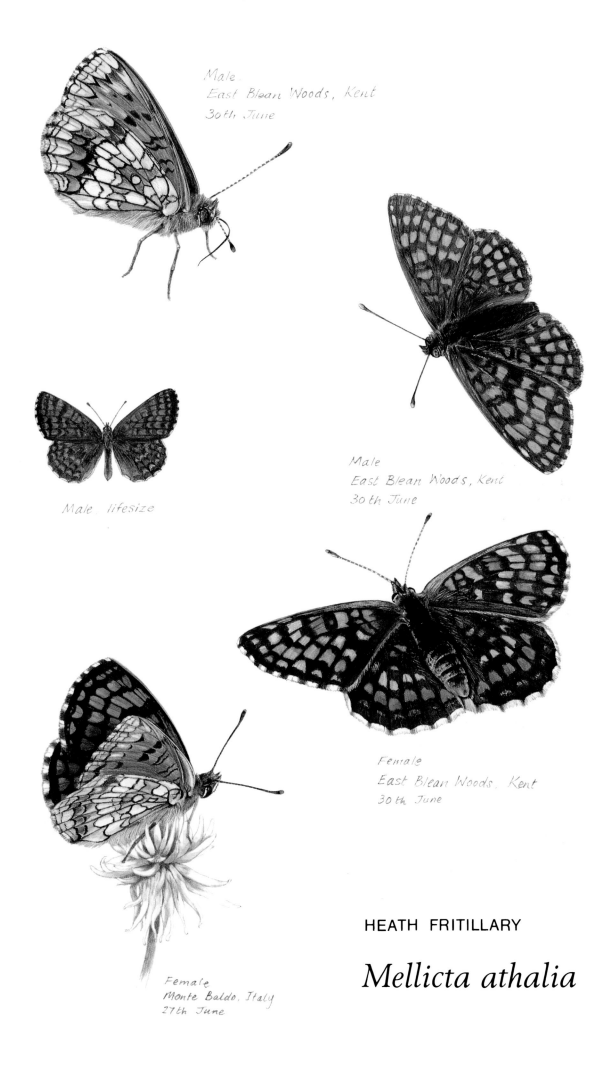

Male.
East Blean Woods, Kent
30th June

Male, lifesize

Male
East Blean Woods, Kent
30th June

Female
East Blean Woods, Kent
30th June

Female
Monte Baldo, Italy
27th June

HEATH FRITILLARY

Mellicta athalia

Female, lifesize

Female

Male

Paintings of Marsh fritillaries
reared in captivity from pupae

Female

Male

MARSH FRITILLARY

Eurodryas aurinia

MARSH FRITILLARY

My first, and only, sighting of the Marsh Fritillary *(Eurodryas aurinia)* in the wild occurred on 18 June 2001 in the foothills of the Spanish Pyrenees. This was a fleeting glimpse, but I had no difficulty in identifying it as I had already made paintings of this Fritillary, based on photographs I had taken several years earlier.

It happened this way. My friend Peter West was, like me, hoping to assemble a collection of slides illustrating each of the butterflies on the British list. When we looked at distribution maps of the Marsh Fritillary, we soon realised that the main focus of this butterfly was in the southwest, and here we were living in the northeast, up in Northumberland. So Peter decided to buy some chrysalids and rear them in his garden shed. Some time later, I got a call from him saying that the butterflies had emerged and would I like to join him in photographing them. It happened to be a lovely, sunny day and we set about taking pictures of the dozen or so Marsh Fritillaries in his garden. I took fourteen good pictures – at least, they would have been good pictures had the butterflies alighted on wildflowers. But no; they persisted in settling on French marigolds – hardly a plant one would associate with the natural habitat of *E. aurinia!*

This Fritillary is found in two different habitats: damp neutral/acidic grassland, or chalk downland, in places where its food plant, devilsbit scabious, grows. These plants must have substantial leaves as the females will only lay their eggs on the undersides of large leaves. The young caterpillars spin a web on which they bask as a group. When they reach their fourth instar and are about three-quarters grown, they make a denser hibernation web where they remain until the following March. The butterflies emerge from their chrysalids in late May or June.

Like most of our other Fritillaries, the Marsh has declined in numbers since the 1940s, mainly due to agricultural 'improvement' of grassland by herbicides, and by drainage. I sometimes wonder whether this butterfly could be reintroduced to a splendid fen nature reserve near where I live in south Norfolk, where devilsbit scabious grows in profusion.

The Marsh Fritillary used to be known as the Greasy Fritillary, and one can imagine that once its colours faded with age, it would remain with a predominantly black network pattern, not at all attractive! My paintings, which illustrate newly-emerged and therefore brightly-coloured butterflies, give some idea of the bold, contrasty design of the Marsh Fritillary. On looking closely at the female, depicted at middle left, I notice that she lacks bold, black dots on the orange patches of the hindwings. This is unusual.

7

Satyridae:

MARBLED WHITE & THE BROWNS

MARBLED WHITE

GRAYLING

SCOTCH ARGUS

MEADOW BROWN

RINGLET

GATEKEEPER

SMALL HEATH

SPECKLED WOOD

WALL

MARBLED WHITE

This butterfly has great beauty within its simple design. It is entirely without bright colours, has no metallic sheen, and lacks cunning camouflage patterns. It stands boldly obvious, having only a few underwing false eye spots to distract a predator. The Marbled White *(Melanargia galathea)*, is also eminently photogenic; the photographer couldn't wish for a better subject. It is not at all camera-shy, and even if it is disturbed whilst nectaring, it will probably merely fly to another flowerhead nearby. The simple colour scheme stands out well against a darker background; and because it likes to bask on long grass stems, it offers the photographer the chance to compose a pleasing picture.

Its generic name *Melanargia*, translated from the Greek, simply means 'black and white' though, paradoxically, it is included in the sub-family *Satyrinae* whose members are almost all brown butterflies! This butterfly prefers chalk downland or limestone areas and it requires grass that is not closely grazed. There seem to be different opinions as to what grasses it uses as a larval food plant. Several have been mentioned including red fescue, sheep's-fescue, tor grass and Yorkshire-fog. The females do not lay their eggs on the food plants, but hover over them and scatter the eggs to fall among the stems. When the larvae hatch, they hide among the vegetation and go into hibernation until the following spring. The Marbled White has one generation a year, the butterflies emerging in late June and flying until mid-August. They live in colonies varying in size from a few dozen to many hundreds.

It is a relief to realise that this is a butterfly whose numbers are stable throughout central Europe, and which appears to be increasing its range in Britain by spreading northwards and eastwards through the English counties.

I have photographed the Marbled White at coastal sites and on downland on the Isle of Wight, at Bernwood Forest near Oxford, and abroad at Brodenbach/Mosel in Germany, and in Lombardia in Italy. Almost all my pictures show it feeding on flowers such as knapweed, clover, creeping thistle, field scabious and globe thistle. Those pictures taken on the Isle of Wight, especially at Compton Down, show several Marbled Whites hosting red mites. These carnivorous parasites are seen clinging to the butterflies, usually around the thorax, sometimes two or three together.

My paintings show that the Marbled White is not simply black and white. The underside of the wings, especially the hindwings of the female, are a pale ochre, and the leading edge of the forewing in the female, when seen from above, bears an ochre tint as it nears the wing root. This can be seen in the illustration at top right.

♀ Bernwood Forest
Oxford
19 July

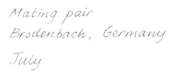

♂ Bernwood Forest, Oxford
19 July

Mating pair
Brodenbach, Germany
July

♀ Lifesize

MARBLED WHITE

Melanargia galathea

Female, lifesize

Female
Holy Island, Northumberland
1st. August

Mating pair
Brightstone, Isle of Wight
27th July

Frost's Common, Norfolk
5th August

West Harling Forest, Norfolk
27th July

GRAYLING

Hipparchia semele

GRAYLING

The Grayling *(Hipparchia semele)* is an old aquaintance of mine from my birding days on Holy Island. Here I used to watch them feeding on ragwort, but more usually basking on the silver sandhills of the dunes. Graylings would often be seen with their wings folded, tilted over on one side. I was told that this was a ploy to minimise their shadows in an attempt to make themselves invisible. I have come to doubt this explanation. I believe that the wing tilting is to maximise the amount of radiant heat from the sun, and thereby retain body heat, and to shield themselves from the cool breeze off the sea.

In contrast to this behaviour, I have noted Rock Grayling *(Hipparchia alcyone)* in the Spanish Pyrenees using its shadow to mimic the countless other shadows cast by a multitude of stones forming the scree on a hillside, and thus making itself difficult to spot. Here the ambient temperature is so high that there is no need for the butterfly to conserve heat!

There is no doubt that the Grayling is a master of camouflage. Nature has provided it with underwing patterns of amazing complexity (as I know only too well when I sit down to paint them!). The mating pair, which I have illustrated at top left opposite, were virtually invisible when seen against the chalky soil and tangle of dead grass in the disused quarry at Brightstone on the Isle of Wight. Similarly, the specimen shown at bottom right was well nigh impossible to detect against the bark of an oak tree. I would never have found it if I hadn't seen it land there!

Looking at recent butterfly distribution maps, one can see that the Grayling has become a mainly coastal butterfly, although its prevalence on dry heathland and in old quarries and other undisturbed places is still well represented. In West Harling Forest I used to find one or two Graylings, as I did in other forests nearby but, sad to say, I haven't seen any during the past six years.

On local, small remaining areas of heathland however, I can still be sure of seeing this intriguing butterfly. On one occasion, about four years ago, I watched the interesting courtship manoeuvres of a pair of Graylings. Of particular note was the manner in which the male closed his wings around the female's antennae, causing her to brush them along his scent glands and release pheromones to encourage her!

The female lays her eggs singly on or near grass leaves: sheep's fescue; bristle bent; or, on the coast, marram grass. Like the Marbled White, the young caterpillar hibernates throughout the winter and resumes feeding in the spring.

SCOTCH ARGUS

I persuaded my wife that it would be a good idea to travel from our home in Northumberland to that butterfly-rich corner of Morecambe Bay where, at Arnside Knott, we would probably find the Scotch Argus *(Erebia aethiops)*. To give ourselves a decent break from our daily chores, we decided to stay overnight at Silverdale on the Lancashire/Cumbria border. This would, perhaps, give us a better chance of finding a spell of sunshine in what had been quite mixed weather.

So, on 29 July 1982 we were walking up the hill at Arnside Knott and along a path which led to an open place where blue moorgrass grows. This dense, tufty grass gave the area a rather odd, hummocky appearance quite unlike any grassland we had seen before. A glance round the sky revealed about five-eighths cloud. Full of excited anticipation, we searched for the sight of a butterfly: had we come all this way for nothing? A beam of bright sunshine traversed the site and, as if by a signal, about twenty dark-brown butterflies appeared from the vegetation, fluttering just above the grass tufts. Some made their way towards the few flowers, mostly hawkweed and procumbent bramble. I prepared myself for photography, realising that it would involve shuffling about on my knees. Suddenly, all the butterflies vanished!

The sun had gone behind a cloud, and the butterflies had dropped into the ground cover. When the sun reappeared, out came the Scotch Arguses again. I have never seen butterflies so photosensitive! Presumably, they conserve body heat by taking shelter with wings closed, until the sun shines again.

The female Scotch Argus lays her eggs after descending deep into the moorgrass and placing her eggs singly on a leaf blade. The young caterpillars, after eating their egg shells on hatching, rest safely during the day in the dense tuft, and at dusk climb up the grass stems to feed. Eventually, they enter hibernation until springtime when they resume feeding.

The only other *Erebia* on the list of British butterflies is the Mountain Ringlet *(Erebia epiphron)* which, sad to say, I have not seen in Britain. Our two representatives of this genus compare poorly with the staggering *thirty-nine Erebia* species found in Europe! All have dark-brown upper wing surfaces with white-pupilled, black eye spots on orange patches, in various permutations. What headaches they must cause for the novice lepidopterist!

Male. lifesize

SCOTCH ARGUS

Erebia aethiops

MEADOW BROWN

Maniola jurtina

Female, lifesize

MEADOW BROWN

The Meadow Brown (*Maniola jurtina*) *is* very widely distributed throughout the British Isles, as it is in Europe. It is Britain's most abundant butterfly, occurring wherever there is unmanaged grassland, not heavily grazed. It is also found along woodland rides, hedges and the verges of country roads, and on heaths and moors. It is absent from the hilly regions of the North, and from intensively-farmed areas. This butterfly also needs a sufficiency of flowers on which to feed. My collection of photographs of the Meadow Brown includes pictures of them nectaring on creeping thistle, knapweed, wild carrot, yarrow, red clover, bramble flowers, ragwort and, in the garden, on buddleia.

The female *jurtina* chooses to lay her very small eggs on fine grasses such as *Poa* and *Agrostis* species, rather than coarse grasses. She may place the eggs precisely on a grass blade, or scatter them in sequence over the tufts at random. The young caterpillars overwinter in the tussocks, eating during mild days but, after hibernating, and after the caterpillars become large enough to attract birds, they resort to feeding at night.

My photographs include pictures of mating Meadow Browns. Like the Whites and most of the Blues, Brown butterflies often mate openly. This may be because they are capable of sufficiently rapid flight when coupled, to allow them to escape attacks by birds or other predators. Certainly, mating Meadow Browns, when disturbed, can fly off in tandem, albeit rather clumsily. Their pre-mating overtures are very brief, the male enveloping the female with aphrodisiac pheromones, and mating soon follows.

On one occasion, I watched a pre-mating couple that appeared to have got themselves into a hopeless tangle! Subsequent examination of a slide which I took at the time shows the following: the female is holding the male's right antenna between her left foreleg and her left antenna; and this complex caressing is being enhanced by the male bending his abdomen round at a right angle to his thorax to touch this antenna/leg/antenna embrace. At the same time, her right antenna is stroking his left antenna! All very passionate, no doubt.

Photographs of paired butterflies are useful in comparing the relative size and underwing markings of the sexes side-by-side. In the Meadow Brown, males and females have a quite different appearance, especially when seen from above. The male is smaller than the female and is much darker. His false eye spots are much less prominent, being surrounded by a mere smudge of orange, whereas the female brightly displays her eye spots at the tips of large bands of orange. There is less difference between the sexes on the undersides, although the female markings are bolder and her false eye marks more prominent. The eye spots are used both as a means of scaring a predator when the forewing is suddenly raised, and also as back-to-front mimicry to distract a predator into believing that the eye mark is at the front end of the butterfly rather than being well away from its vital parts.

RINGLET

When carrying out regular patrols of my patch in West Harling Forest, I sometimes find myself being taken unawares by the emergence of the Ringlet *(Aphantopus hyperantus)*. The dark-brown male Ringlet closely resembles the male Meadow Brown, which is on the wing about a fortnight before the first male Ringlets appear at the end of June, and I tend to regard the new arrivals as just more male Meadow Browns. Soon, there is no doubt whatsoever, as the forest rides become home to hundreds of Ringlets. Their eye spots on the underwings seem to stare at one from every flower. Heads of creeping thistle, knapweed, ragwort, viper's bugloss and bramble flowers are soon covered by nectaring butterflies: Meadow Browns, Ringlets and, a week or so later, Gatekeepers.

My logbook entries indicate the swelling numbers of Ringlets throughout July with the word 'several' being replaced by 'many', then by 'abundant' and, in some years, 'super-abundant', the word I use to indicate thousands. In the year 2000, I was recording Ringlets as abundant (hundreds) as early as 27 June, but by 27 July reduced numbers were being recorded as 'many' (about fifty), and by 11 August 'several' (less than ten). Finally, on 16 August, my comment was 'Ringlet: 2 very faded'. The Meadow Browns and Gatekeepers soldier on until September.

Because the Ringlet is an attractive butterfly with its tidy underwing design and glaring eye spots, I have accumulated over fifty close-up photographs of *hyperantus*, including shots of a few aberrant forms. In the course of taking these pictures I have come to realise how prone this butterfly is to predation by spiders. I have several pictures of Ringlets' wing parts and skeletal remains within spiders' webs. Many of the ragwort flowerheads are interlaced with webs and I have found as many as five spider's 'larders' on a single ragwort plant.

The Ringlet is widespread in many parts of Britain, though not as ubiquitous as the Meadow Brown. It appears to shun industrial areas and mountainous regions, but is well represented on downland, on woodland rides and edges, and along the borders of lanes and hedgerows. Its vernacular name 'Ringlet' is derived from its prominent eye spots. When seen in plan view, the adults seem to be almost black when they first appear, and there seems to be little difference between the sexes, but as they age, they assume a more chocolate-brown colour, and the female is seen to be slightly lighter coloured than the male, particularly on the undersides. When oblique sunshine strikes the undersides, the light catches raised features such as the wing veins, which take on a golden gleam. The bold eye spots present a number of potential targets for a predatory bird, as can be judged from the Ringlets seen with tattered wings. This is quite a sturdy butterfly, however. It is often seen flying on dull days, in inclement weather and even in the rain!

Aphantopus hyperantus

Lifesize

Male

Female

Mating pair
East Harling, Norfolk
10th July

Female
West Harling Forest, Norfolk
18th July

Male
East Harling, Norfolk
20th July

Female
East Harling, Norfolk
18th July

Female, lifesize

Female
West Harling Forest, Norfolk
13th August

Male
West Harling Forest, Norfolk
18th July

Male
West Harling Forest, Norfolk
3rd August

Mating pair
Ickworth, Suffolk
27th July

GATEKEEPER

Pyronia tithonus

GATEKEEPER

The name 'Gatekeeper', or its alternative, Hedge Brown, are suggestive of the traditional English countryside when farm gates were set in hedges beside unclipped grass verges, where wildflowers grew and butterflies brought extra colour and movement to the rural scene. The scientific name, *Pyronia tithonus*, has no such allusion, being derived from the Greek word *purōpos*, meaning fiery-eyed, and *Tithonus*, a Trojan youth beloved by Aurora, the goddess of the dawn (from A. Maitland Emmet in *The Scientific Names of the British Lepidoptera*).

I have always regarded the Gatekeeper as a neat and tidy sort of butterfly. When seen in company with other Brown butterflies that are found along the forest rides in July and August, the Gatekeeper is the brightest, with its striking orange patches above, and its pale ochre flash on the underwing. Moreover, it appears a couple of weeks later than the Meadow Brown and Ringlet and so is brand-new when they may be looking slightly faded. This is a butterfly that I never saw when I lived in Northumberland but, during the past sixteen years, I have recorded and photographed it throughout its flight period in West Harling Forest and at several other woods and fens in the neighbourhood.

My records from the forest show that it has been remarkably consistent in timing its appearance (14,15 or 16 July) and in most years it is seen until the third week in August. Its emergence is heralded with the sight of one or two males, followed by a few more on succeeding days. Their presence precedes the females by several days, allowing the males to establish territories, and hold themselves ready to chase females. Mating takes place soon after the females emerge. The mating I have illustrated in my paintings took place against an aristocratic background on the estate of Ickworth House in Suffolk, on 27 July 1985.

It is quite easy to distinguish male from female Gatekeepers, especially when they are basking in the sunshine with their wings wide open, something they do frequently. The male has heavy, dark smudges across his forewings extending diagonally from the bottom edge up towards the eye spot at the apex. These dark marks are sex brands – dense collections of androconial cells which are absent in the female. Otherwise, both sexes have similar patterns, though the female is noticeably larger than the male.

The female scatters her eggs over suitable clumps of grass, such as bents and fescues, or meadow grass, sited in sunny places. The caterpillar, after eating its egg shell and shedding its first skin, goes into hibernation until early spring when it feeds nocturnally on the newly-growing grass tips.

In Britain, the Gatekeeper is a southern butterfly being, in the main, confined to lowlands south of a line from the Cumbrian coast across to the estuary of the river Tees. The intensification of agriculture and removal of many hedges in recent years has been responsible for some reduction in its numbers. On the other hand, since the early 1980s, it has extended its range northwards and in the central counties of Leicestershire, Nottinghamshire and Derbyshire.

SMALL HEATH

his small, inconspicuous butterfly has been extraordinarily successful in colonising most of mainland Britain. Its habitats are diverse: it can be found in large numbers on heaths, on downland, among coastal dunes, and in smaller numbers on woodland rides, waste ground and roadside verges. It requires grassland that is composed of fine, short grasses on well-drained land. The Small Heath *(Coenonympha pamphilus)* is easily recognised by its seemingly erratic, jinking flight during which it reveals its golden colour with every wing beat. It seldom flies high or far, and is often seen at its most vigorous when defending its territory. I have often watched a male actively preserving its ownership of a lookout point, which may be on a low shrub or even a particular spot on the ground. Males also go on brief reconnaissance flights between their periods of guard duty. The females are more sedentary, and venture into male territory only when they are ready to mate.

In West Harling Forest, the Small Heaths have two broods in most years, though they are not clearly defined as there is considerable overlapping of broods. The butterflies which appear in May have emerged from chrysalids formed from caterpillars which spent the winter in hibernation. The July/August butterflies are from caterpillars pupating in June, although some of them will not pupate, but will go into hibernation and produce next year's early butterflies.

My logbook shows that I usually record my first sighting of *pamphilus* in May (in 1990 as early as 5 May) and in some years my final sighting is as late as October. I rarely see many Small Heaths at one time during my transect walks – never more than a dozen, and usually only two or three. Although the sandy soil is well drained, there are not enough large areas of suitable fine grasses to allow large colonies to develop.

The Small Heath is not an easy butterfly to photograph. It is small; spends much of its time resting low down among the grasses and small plants of the forest rides; will not open its wings except when flying; and even when it decides to feed from a flower, it will choose a low-growing plant such as clover or wild strawberry. So, the photographer is obliged to kneel to get a good close-up picture. The butterfly, however, does not take kindly to a human being kneeling alongside it, and clears off! Sometimes one finds Small Heaths nectaring on taller plants such as ragwort, as I did when taking the photographs on which my paintings are based. On this occasion, on Wortham Ling Common near Diss, I came across about twenty Small Heaths feeding among clumps of ragwort and was able to take many pictures.

In my paintings, I have not indicated the sex of the butterflies shown in the larger illustrations. This is because the sexes are similar with few distinguishing features. I am pretty certain, however, that the painting at top left is a male, the other three being females.

West Harling, Norfolk
12th June

Male, lifesize

Wortham Ling Common
Diss, Norfolk

31 August

Wortham Ling Common
Diss, Norfolk
31 August

West Tofts Heath, Norfolk
6 June 1988

SMALL HEATH

Coenonympha pamphilus

Frosts Common
Great Hookham, Norfolk
5th August

East Harling, Norfolk
7th September

Female, lifesize

SPECKLED WOOD

Pararge aegeria

East Harling, Norfolk
15th June

West Harling Forest, Norfolk
15th June

SPECKLED WOOD

The Speckled Wood *(Pararge aegeria)* is easily identified, with its almost checkerboard pattern of pale-yellow patches on a dark-chocolate ground. At least, this is its appearance when seen resting with open wings. On the underside, the forewing more or less repeats the pattern of the topside, but the underside of the hindwing is more cryptic in design and provides excellent camouflage when the butterfly is roosting with its wings closed and its forewings retracted. Interestingly, the colour of the wing patches varies from white at the northern limit of its range, to bright orange at its southernmost locations in the Mediterranean regions.

Pararge aegeria is a shade-loving butterfly. Its colouring and pattern harmonises with the dappled light of broad leaved woodland or at the edge of conifer plantations. Unlike the Fritillaries, which have sadly declined in numbers since the practice of coppicing has declined, the Speckled Wood has benefited from reduced woodland management.

This butterfly gets most of its sustenance from the aphid honeydew which covers the leaf surfaces of oak, ash or birch but, when the honeydew declines in late summer, both males and females take nectar from flowerheads, especially ragwort. Over the years, I have taken forty-six photographs of the Speckled Wood and only two show the butterfly on flowers, one on ragwort and the other on creeping thistle. Another picture shows a male courting a female, and yet another shows a Speckled Wood in the grip of a crab spider. In the remaining forty-two pictures the butterflies are seen resting, or guarding a favourite patch of sunshine. Most of them are perched on bramble leaves or nettle; others are on the leaves of lime, willow, beech, bracken or bindweed.

Despite the fact that we see Speckled Woods sitting in a patch of sunlight on low woodland foliage, a place a male will stoutly defend against any intruder, it should be remembered that many, perhaps the bulk of a given colony, may be flitting about the high canopy. It is likely that much of the mating takes place among the treetops. A male butterfly, getting bored with the prospect of waiting for a female to visit his sunlit bower near ground level, will fly up to the canopy to look for a mate. Thus one often notices patrolling males prospecting at all levels.

I make my regular counts of butterfly numbers by walking a transect along two connecting rides in the forest – in all about 3 kilometres. I note butterflies seen along the rides and on either side to a width of about 5 metres. This method is perfectly satisfactory when counting most species but, in the case of the Speckled Wood, I can only include those seen on the lower foliage and therefore I have no way of knowing the true numbers of Speckled Woods present. However, my records give some indication of the duration of *aegeria's* presence. In 1999, for example, I first saw Speckled Wood on 28 April; on four visits during May; on seven visits during June; five times in July; four times in August, including a count of more than thirty butterflies; and twice in September, including a count of thirty-six.

WALL

The patterning of the Wall butterfly *(Lasiommata megera)* bears a resemblance to that of the Speckled Wood except that, whereas the latter may be regarded as having pale spots on a brown background, the Wall appears to have brown tracery on a golden background. Superficially, the Wall might be taken for a Fritillary, but the large eye spots mark it out as a Brown butterfly, a member of the family *Satyridae*. There need be no struggle in deciding the sex of a Wall: the male is easily identified by the broad, dark sex brands traversing the forewings diagonally in the direction of the eye spot at the apex. This is absent in the female. The underside of the hindwings of both sexes is a wonderful tapestry of zig-zags and eye spots, though with a dull overall colour scheme. This affords the butterflies good camouflage when resting with closed wings, or when mating (as shown in the painting opposite).

The Wall is often seen with its wings wide open, basking in the sunshine. This is done to keep its thoracic flight muscles at a sufficiently high temperature for them to provide instant power for a rapid take-off should the need arise. It receives heat in two ways: direct heat from the sun's rays on its wing surfaces, and reflected heat from the warm ground. This is the reason for its perching on a sunny wall surface with its wings closed, the envelope of closed wings retaining its body heat and its underparts receiving warmth from the wall surface. Indeed, one of my first photographs of *megera* shows it perched on a whitewashed wall in full sun! Of course, the Wall butterfly is not alone in practising thermoregulation in this way – all butterflies do it – but the Wall prefers open spaces, where cool winds may soon reduce body heat.

The Wall is found in many different open situations: woodland edges, roadside verges, hedgerows, and I have found them in West Harling Forest on the sides of the earthen fire-breaks which divide plantations. Here, the embankments give shelter and provide suntraps. The males are often seen patrolling along these fire-breaks, searching for mates. The gravid female lays her eggs singly in sheltered depressions on bare ground, or directly onto grass tufts on broken ground, sheltered by nearby shrubs or young conifers. There are usually two broods a year, the early butterflies appearing in mid-May to mid-June, and their progeny are seen on the wing in August. Apart from small numbers of Wall butterflies seen among the fire-breaks, my records for West Harling Forest are meagre. They occur much more frequently in other woods in the neighbourhood. When we lived in Northumberland, *megera* was a regular companion in the garden. We were ideally placed, as they bred among a complex of hedges and broken ground just beyond our back garden.

Female
West Harling Forest, Norfolk
3 June

Female
Ponteland, Northumberland
9 June

Male
West Harling Forest
31 May

Mating pair
Hickling Broad, Norfolk
8 June

Female, lifesize

WALL

Lasiommata megera

8

Hesperiidae:

SKIPPERS

GRIZZLED SKIPPER

DINGY SKIPPER

LULWORTH SKIPPER

ESSEX SKIPPER

SMALL SKIPPER

SILVER-SPOTTED SKIPPER

LARGE SKIPPER

GRIZZLED SKIPPER

The Grizzled Skipper *(Pyrgus malvae)* looks quite different from any other butterfly seen in the British Isles, though the Latticed Heath moth could be mis-identified as one. In Europe, however, there are no less than twenty-three Grizzled Skipper lookalikes. Some are slightly bigger, but all have the same blackish-brown ground colour scattered with small, white patches, and all have dark and light striped fringes to their wings. It requires keen eyesight and wide knowledge to be able to sort them out. Thankfully, we don't have this challenge. We should, however, be quite concerned at the decline of the Grizzled Skipper in England.

This butterfly is found on woodland rides, chalk grassland, abandoned railway tracks and sometimes on coastal dunes and heathland. It requires sufficient nectaring plants to provide energy for its vigorous flight, and appropriate plants on which its caterpillars can feed. In our local forest at West Harling, the Grizzled skipper caterpillar food plant is wild strawberry which is widespread, though low-growing bramble may also be used.

Eggs are laid singly, usually on plants in a sunny situation growing among low vegetation with patches of bare ground. The butterfly is first seen on the wing in late April (much earlier than the 'golden' skippers). It flies until mid-July and, in some places, there is a second brood in August. One reads of huge colonies of over a hundred butterflies, but in West Harling Forest I regarded myself lucky to see ten in one day. My first local record in the forest was on 9 May 1987 when I counted eight along a south-facing ride, where they were feeding on ground ivy, dandelion and buttercup. A week later, on the same ride, I noted ten Grizzled Skippers, one of which was fighting a Dingy Skipper. Ten days after that I could find only two. The years 1988–93 yielded similar small numbers, rarely outlasting May, and apart from a single sighting in 1995 and one in 2000, I have seen no others. Of course, the forest covers a large area and there may be colonies in other parts, but other people have searched for the Grizzled Skipper in the forest with little success.

The Grizzled Skipper is a delightful little butterfly which, if not resting, seems to be restlessly darting about on urgent business. There is little difference in appearance between the sexes; their behaviour is probably the best indicator of their sex. The males pugnaciously attack almost any passing insect, while the females are more sedentary, only flying now and again to feed or to seek out suitable plants on which to lay their eggs.

Male, lifesize

West Harling Forest, Norfolk
23rd May

West Harling Forest
21st May

West Harling Forest
5th May

GRIZZLED SKIPPER

Pyrgus malvae

West Harling Forest
16th May

West Harling Forest, Norfolk
20th May

Female, lifesize

Male, West Harling Forest, Norfolk
23rd May

Female, West Harling Forest
31st May

Female, West Harling Forest
9th June

DINGY SKIPPER

Erynnis tages

DINGY SKIPPER

The Dingy Skipper *(Erynnis tages)* is aptly named in that, apart from some pale pinkish-fawn, sepia and dark-brown patterns which decorate the upper surfaces of its forewings, the hindwings and undersides are decidedly drab, relieved only by a scattering of small white spots. When it is resting on the ground among a litter of dead grasses and dried leaves, it may be overlooked. Perhaps this is the purpose of its inconspicuous colouring!

This is the most wide-ranging of our Skipper butterflies, though its colonies are often quite small. It is found in many parts of southern England from Cornwall across to Kent and up into the Midlands, Derbyshire, Yorkshire and County Durham. It is also present in North and South Wales, in Ireland, and on the Moray Firth in northern Scotland. Sad to say, it is poorly represented in East Anglia.

I became acquainted with the Dingy Skipper when living in Northumberland. My friend Peter West had heard about a colony of these Skippers at Waldridge Fell, near Chester-le-Street in County Durham and, during one bright morning in May 1982 Peter and I, with our wives, made the short journey south to look for Dingy Skippers. Waldridge Fell is a large expanse of unimproved grassland near the village of Waldridge and it is used as a recreation area for dog-walkers, children's games, kite-flying and other outdoor activities. It is in no sense a park; there are no manicured lawns or tidy flower beds.

In places it is covered with large patches of common bird's-foot trefoil and smaller patches of silverweed, and is also dotted with plantains and knapweed. Bare areas of dark soil suggest slag from a former pit heap. There were many Dingy Skippers about, almost all resting on the ground. Among the dozen or so photographs I took at the time, one shows a female skipper ovipositing on a trefoil leaf, with an egg clearly seen nearby. Another shot shows a Dingy Skipper resting on a dead stalk with its wings drooping and looking rather like a half-closed umbrella!

More recently, I have photographed this Skipper on the Isle of Wight, and in our local forest at West Harling. Here we have seen a sad decline of the Dingy Skipper. During the years 1986–91, I recorded sightings between mid-May and mid-June; not large numbers, but sufficient to give assurance that we might have a permanent colony. Alas, apart from a single sighting on 3 June 1993, the Dingy Skipper has not been seen since. Why this has happened, I do not know. The Dingy Skipper's larval food plant, common bird's-foot trefoil, still grows on the forest rides, though not as widely as it did a decade ago. What I and others find particularly depressing is that the disappearance of this butterfly almost exactly coincides with the disappearance of the Grizzled Skipper from the same parts of the forest.

LULWORTH SKIPPER

My first encounter with the Lulworth Skipper *(Thymelicus acteon)* occurred in August 1991 during a holiday in Dorset and Hampshire, where my wife and I hoped to follow our respective interests – country houses and butterfly hunting. I was watching a number of Small Skippers *(Thymelicus sylvestris)* feeding on a patch of spear thistles and smooth hawksbeard beside a rough track leading down to the rock formation of Durdle Door, near the village of Lulworth. The Small Skippers were reaching the end of their flight period, it being mid-August, and had lost many of their golden scales, appearing drab and faded. Looking more closely, I realised that there were other, darker, Skippers among the group of feeding butterflies and eventually I spotted the golden 'sun-ray' markings which denote a female Lulworth Skipper.

It took me much longer to find a male among the throng of Small Skippers. Eventually, it was the darker colouring and the very prominent dark sex brands on the wings of the male that helped me to sort them out. So I began to photograph what I believed to be Lulworth Skippers. However, despite my firm conviction that I now knew one species from the other, I was disappointed to find that, when my slides were returned from processing and I was able to study them in detail, I had photographed nine Lulworth Skippers and, mistakenly, seven Small Skippers!

Later in the week, after we had visited several stately homes, we went further west along the coast to Burton Bradstock where I found a small colony of *acteon*. I took more photographs on a new film at Burton but my attempts to get more pictures were foiled when I discovered that a small piece of grit had prevented my camera back from closing properly, and the whole film was fogged. Alas, the fates had not finished their pranks! Joan tumbled on a rough, stony track and sprained her ankle, thus curtailing what was intended to be a happy holiday.

Lulworth skippers fly only when the sun shines, and spend dull days hiding among the tufts of tall grass. The females are extremely selective when laying their eggs, using only the tall tor-grass. When finding a suitable flower sheath the female will descend it, moving backwards down the sheath, and carefully deposit her clutch of eggs in a row. When the eggs hatch, the young caterpillar eats some of its eggshell and then spins a cocoon around itself and the remains of the eggshell. Here it will hibernate until the following spring.

The *acteon* populations in Dorset remain fairly constant, as they do in southern Europe, but the species has suffered a severe decline in the north of the Continent. When I was in the Spanish Pyrenees in late June 2001, I was able to photograph a Lulworth Skipper which had extremely bright sun-ray marks, leaving one in no doubt as to the species. I could have saved a good deal of film if the Dorset ones had been as bright!

Female
Durdle Door, Dorset
12 August

Male
Durdle Door, Dorset
12 August

Lifesize

Female

Male

Female
Durdle Door, Dorset
12 August

Male
Purbeck Hills, Dorset
14 August

LULWORTH SKIPPER

Thymelicus acteon

Male. lifesize

Female
West Harling Forest, Norfolk
7th July

West Harling Forest, Norfolk
17th July

Male
Great Hockham, Norfolk
25th July

Male, West Harling Forest, Norfolk
1st August

ESSEX SKIPPER

Thymelicus lineola

ESSEX SKIPPER

From mid-June to mid-August the rides which constitute my study area in West Harling Forest abound with Skipper butterflies, and throughout July many thousands of them are on the wing whenever the weather is suitable. These Skippers are: Essex Skipper *(Thymelicus lineola)*; Small Skipper; and, in smaller numbers, Large Skipper. Two of these, Essex and Small, resemble each other very closely and defy rapid, positive indentification. For many years butterfly collectors were unaware that these look-alike butterflies were of different species. Indeed, it was not until 1906 that *lineola* was named 'Essex Skipper'.

What is the best way of sorting them out? Well, one can capture an Essex and a Small Skipper and examine their genitalia through a microscope, refer to illustrations in a textbook, and decide which is which! But what is the best way to differentiate them in the field? There are three things to look for: first, look at the colour of the underside of the tips of their antennae – if they are jet black then you are looking at an Essex Skipper; if they are orange or beige, you have a Small Skipper. Secondly, look at the upper surfaces of the wings – if you can see a dark sex brand in the centre of each wing, you are looking at a male butterfly. Then see if the sex brand is running parallel with the leading edge of the wing and is about 2.5 millimetres long. If it is, you have an Essex Skipper (see bottom two paintings opposite). If the sex brand is long (about 4 millimetres) and is slightly curved and not parallel to the wing's leading edge, you are looking at a Small Skipper (see the upper left painting of the Small Skipper on p.135). Thirdly, look at the underside of the butterfly's forewing – if it is a uniform orange colour, it belongs to an Essex Skipper. If it shades gradually to a lighter, greyish colour at the wingtip, it belongs to a Small Skipper. Practise these observations for several years, and you will know the difference between an Essex and a Small Skipper at a glance! I have been using these methods for about fifteen years, and I still make mistakes.

Records taken on my patch in the forest show that the Essex Skipper usually appears in the first week of July, a week or ten days after I first see the Small Skipper. Soon its numbers earn the classification 'abundant', and a few days later I record 'super-abundant'. Everywhere I look, each flowerhead is garlanded with Skippers feeding on scabious, knapweed, ragwort and especially viper's bugloss, which attracts the greatest numbers. In some places I find that all the Skippers are Essex, probably near a breeding site used annually. When not feeding, the butterflies are often seen perched on the heads of grass, and one can approach them closely.

The angles at which they hold their wings is interesting. The hindwings are held flat and the forewings are set to form a V just above the hindwings, thus producing pockets of warmth when they bask in the sun. This, together with their very hairy body, provides their flight muscles with ample heat to allow instant flight should danger arise, and maintain rapid darting flight when airborne.

SMALL SKIPPER

Looking through my large collection of butterfly slides, I was surprised to discover that I have accumulated no less than seventy-two pictures of the Small Skipper *(Thymelicus sylvestris)*. These illustrate the butterfly feeding, courting, mating and being preyed on by crab spiders. They also demonstrate the value of using the underside of the forewings as a recognition feature. Many of my slides show clearly the pale grey shading on the tips of the forewing underside. This shading does not occur on the look-alike Essex Skipper. Some of the slides give a good illustration of how the Small Skippers feed communally, apparently without squabbling. I have two slides showing five Skippers feeding side-by-side on a single knapweed flower.

My logbook shows that, over the last decade, my first sightings of the Small Skipper are occurring earlier, dropping from 15 July in 1990 to 22 June in 1999, although my last sightings remain more or less stable at around 20 August. The range of the butterfly in England has been steadily increasing northwards. When I lived in Northumberland up to 1984, I had never seen a Skipper butterfly of any kind. Looking at the distribution map in *The Millennium Atlas of Butterflies in Britain and Ireland* I am glad to see that, during the past few years, the Small Skipper has now reached that county.

The preferred caterpillar food plant of the Small Skipper is the grass Yorkshire fog growing tall in ungrazed places. The female lays her eggs in a leaf sheath, slowly backing down and inserting the base of her abdomen into the sheath and placing her eggs therein. When the eggs hatch, the young caterpillar first eats its eggshell before spinning a small cocoon and settling down to hibernate until the spring. When it beomes active again it starts to eat the wall of the sheath before emerging to gorge on tender leaves near at hand. It then becomes independent but still protecting itself by constructing further tubes from rolled grass leaves, within which to eat until June, when it descends to the base of the grass clump where it forms a chrysalis.

Small Skippers are remarkable flyers. The males particularly spend much of their time in sunny weather jinking over the flowers, their wings flashing gold as the sunlight catches them. In West Harling Forest they feed on scabious, knapweed, spear thistle, ragwort and viper's bugloss. When they have claimed a female, they are seen mating quite openly, resting on bracken or the flowerheads of grasses.

Male
West Harling Forest, Norfolk
24th July

Male, lifesize

Male
West Harling Forest
7th August

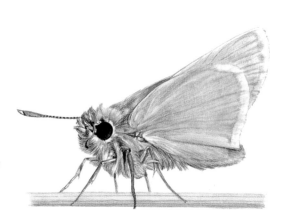

Female
West Harling Forest
18th July

Female.
Barnbow, Leeds, Yorkshire
12th August

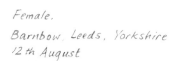

SMALL SKIPPER

Thymelicus sylvestris

Beacon Hill, Warnford,
Hampshire
19 August 1991

Female, lifesize

Female
Beacon Hill, Warnford
19 August 1991

Male
Beacon Hill, Warnford
19 August 1991

SILVER-SPOTTED SKIPPER

Hesperia comma

Female
Beacon Hill, Warnford
19 August 1991

SILVER-SPOTTED SKIPPER

Imagine a beautiful, sunny day in August with a pleasant warmth on one's back as one looks upon a wonderful chalk hillside, with patches of wildflowers nodding in the light southerly breeze. This is my recollection of Beacon Hill, near Winchester, on the day when I first saw the Silver-spotted Skipper *(Hesperia comma)*. My wife and I had been admiring the beauty of Winchester Cathedral and its adjacent buildings during the morning, and then had driven southeast to Warnford and Beacon Hill.

As I picked my way down the escarpment, I saw two fellows whose movements suggested that they might be looking for butterflies. I asked them if I would find Silver-spotted Skippers hereabouts, and they told me to take care because I may be standing on them! There they were, basking on bare chalk patches, or nectaring on flowers among clumps of sheep's fescue. Within minutes, my camera at the ready, I spotted a female Skipper on the point of laying an egg on a blade of fescue, almost under my feet. Unfortunately, a gangling, sniffing dog interrupted my photography, and the butterfly's egg-laying! In about fifteen minutes I had taken eleven shots, being fortunate enough to take close-up pictures of both males and females, seen from above and from the side. Some are shown feeding on field scabious, and some on ox-eye daisies. All the butterflies are seen to be in excellent condition.

The Silver-spotted Skipper, with smart white patches on both surfaces of its wings, is probably our most attractive Skipper, apart, perhaps, from the Chequered Skipper *(Carterocephalus palaemon)* which I have never seen, not having had the opportunity to visit its Scottish strongholds. *Hesperia comma* gets its specific name *comma* from the bold, curved sex brands on the upper forewings of the male, which run from the wing root towards the wing's apex (see painting at lower left). With some imagination, these could be described as comma-shaped, but not nearly so convincingly as the white comma marks on the Comma butterfly. In size and general design, the Silver-spotted Skipper is similar to the Large Skipper.

As intimated above, the food plant of the Silver-spotted Skipper is sheep's fescue. The butterfly breeds only in places where this grows, and only if it is present in small tufts. Eggs are laid singly, usually on tufts close to bare areas of soil. The caterpillars hatch out early in spring and shelter beneath a canopy of grass blades spun together, coming out at night to feed. When the caterpillar is fully grown it pupates close to the ground in a cocoon made from grass and silk. There is one brood a year, the butterflies emerging at the beginning of August. They are seen flying until mid-September.

LARGE SKIPPER

I always look forward to seeing my first Large Skipper of the year. This is the earliest of the 'golden' skippers to appear, and it heralds the coming of large numbers of butterflies that will occupy the forest rides in the summer months. Its scientific name is *Ochlodes venatus* (nowadays written *venata*) and the generic part of the name, *Ochlodes*, comes from the Greek and means 'turbulent' or 'unruly'. The Essex and Small Skippers, which appear a few weeks later than the Large Skipper, could perhaps be described as turbulent when they emerge in hordes in July, but this is not a characteristic of the Large Skipper which appears in fewer numbers. It is true that male Large Skippers sometimes squabble over a lookout position or dash rapidly to chase away a rival, but they never strike me as being turbulent or unruly.

Looking through my records of Large Skipper sightings in West Harling Forest since 1990, I note that the earliest sighting was on 1 June 1999, with the average first sightings being about halfway through June, and last records being dated in early August.

My collection of slides showing the Large Skipper in the field mostly depict it resting on leaves of one sort or another; others show these butterflies feeding on a variety of flowers, including tufted vetch, meadow vetchling, clover, kidney vetch, knapweed, field scabious, bramble and on a hawkweed flower in the centre of which a crab spider is lurking! One delightful picture shows a mating pair of Large Skippers using the voluminous flower of hedge bindweed as their nuptial couch.

The Large Skipper has more patterning on its wings than the Small or Essex Skippers, in whose company it is often seen. The bulbous, dark sex brand on the male's upper wing clearly differentiates the sexes (see the painting at top right, compared with the one at bottom left). On the undersides, the wings are seen to have greenish-brown markings.

This butterfly makes a perfect photographer's model. A resting Large Skipper perched on a leaf can be approached quite closely; using a macro lens about 25 centimetres away from the butterfly will produce a close-up portrait showing every detail. Its very hairy thorax and abdomen, in conjunction with the set of its wings, provide the wing muscles with sufficient conserved heat to launch it into flight in microseconds!

The larval food plants of the Large Skipper are the grasses cocksfoot and false-brome which grow freely in our local forest. It is likely that this butterfly suffers less from changes in forest management than do the short-grass species which are more easily shaded out by quick-growing conifers.

Male, lifesize

Male
West Harling Forest, Norfolk
11 July

West Harling Forest, Norfolk
15 June

Male
Great Hockham, Norfolk
7 July

Female
West Harling Forest
30 June

LARGE SKIPPER

Ochlodes venatus

Bibliography

Here and there in the text of this book, I have quoted short extracts from butterfly textbooks. Indeed, over the years, I have found much useful information in my collection of reference books and field guides. Not only have I been able to glean up-to-date facts concerning the distribution of butterflies, their habitats and their life-cycles, but I have learned much about the behaviour of butterflies. Often, I have been able to verify my reading by observations in the field and, occasionally, I have noted behavioural phenomena not reported in the literature. When working on the paintings for this book, I have been able to use several of the excellent field guides to check details of wing patterns, colouring and variations of the species illustrated. Here is my book list:

Asher, J., Warren, M., Fox, R. *et al. The Millennium Atlas of Butterflies in Britain and Ireland*. OUP, Oxford 2001.

Bristow, C.R., Mitchell, S.H., Bolton, D.E. *Devon Butterflies*. Devon Books, Tiverton, 1993.

Brooks, M., Knight, C. *A Complete Guide to British Butterflies*. Jonathan Cape, London, 1982.

Carter, D. *Butterflies*. Elm Tree Books/British Museum (Natural History), London, 1988.

Chinery, M. *Butterflies and Day-flying Moths of Britain and Europe*. Collins, London, 1989.

Chinery, M. *Butterflies of Britain and Europe*. Harper Collins, London, 1998.

Dal, B. *The Butterflies of Northern Europe*. Croom Helm, London, 1982.

Feltwell, J. *The Natural History of Butterflies*. Croom Helm, Beckenham, 1986.

Ford, E.B. *Butterflies*. Collins, London, 1977.

Goodden, R. *British Butterflies*. David & Charles, Newton Abbot, 1978.

Hall, M.R. *An Atlas of Norfolk Butterflies 1984–1988*. Butterfly Conservation, Norwich, 1991.

Heath, J., Pollard, E., Thomas, J.A. *Atlas of Butterflies in Britain & Ireland*. Viking, Harmondsworth, 1984.

Howarth, T.G. *Butterflies of the British Isles*. Viking, Harmondsworth, 1984.

Maitland Emmet, A., Heath, J. *Butterflies of Great Britain & Ireland*. Harley Books, Colchester, 1990.

Maitland Emmet, A. *The Scientific Names of British Lepidoptera*. Harley Books, Colchester, 1991.

Mendel, H., Piotrowski, S.H. *The Butterflies of Suffolk*. Suffolk Naturalists Society, Ipswich, 1986.

Sandars, E. *A Butterfly Book for the Pocket*. OUP, London, 1939.

Steel, S., Steel, D. *Butterflies of Berkshire, Buckinghamshire & Oxfordshire*. Pisces, Oxford, 1985.

Stewart, A.M. *British Butterflies*. A&C Black, London, 1918.

Thomas, J.A. *RSNC Guide to Butterflies of the British Isles*. Country Life Books, London, 1986.

Thomas, J.A., Lewington, R. *The Butterflies of Britain & Ireland*. Dorling Kindersley, London, 1991.

Tolman, T., Lewington, R. *Butterflies of Britain & Europe*. Harper Collins, London, 1997.

Whalley, P. *Butterfly Watching*. Severn House Publishers Ltd., London, 1980.

Whalley, P. *The Mitchell Beazley Pocket Guide to Butterflies*. Mitchell Beazley, London, 1981.